A Candle on the Hill

A Candle on the Hill

Images of Camphill Life

With a foreword by Sir Laurens van der Post

Edited by Cornelius Pietzner

Anthroposophic Press
Floris Books

First Published in 1990
Reprinted with corrections 1991

© Cornelius Pietzner, 1990
Floris Books, 15 Harrisson Gardens, Edinburgh.
Anthroposophic Press Inc., RR4, Box 94A1, Hudson, NY 12534.

The publication of this book has been supported by
the Thomas Weihs Trust, Great Britain, and
the Camphill Foundation, United States

British Library CIP Data available

ISBN 0–86315–100–0 (hardback)
ISBN 0–86315–101–9 (paperback)

Printed in Great Britain
by BPCC Paulton Books Ltd, Bristol

Contents

Camphill and the shadow of our time

Sir Laurens van der Post

I seem to have been aware most of my life of a strange unease creeping into the spirit of our time, and increasing steadily until it is not only in the basements of our being, but mounting upwards towards the attics of our minds. I suspect that all ages have had to deal with their own peculiar forms of unrest, and that unrest of this kind has somehow to do with the fact that consciousness, which is so young in the evolution of life, is based on choice and discrimination. It cannot deal simultaneously with all the perceptions and intimations of reality constantly clamouring at its door for recognition. In the interests of articulation and communication, not only with man's inmost self but with his neighbours and the world, he has to choose . . . and in the choosing, reject.

Each civilization whose ruins litter the past has followed the reality of its choice and, within that particular favoured field of its awareness, excelled and done more than the cultures that preceded it. But always in the accomplishment of this achievement, what has had to be rejected of all the other infinite aspects, possibilities, and longings in life and creation, accompany it rather like a shadow . . . small at the high noon of achievement and almost eliminated around the heels of what is conscious, but from then on lengthening quickly until at sunset it is long and striding high and wide and often diabolically compelling as it meets the night — the giant night from which the first light of consciousness was stolen.

Jung once referred to this specifically when he told me that the thing one sacrifices in accomplishing a particular aspect of oneself returns, as it were, knife in hand, one day to sacrifice that which sacrificed it within us. In this sense, shadow and unease are both witness and warning, both of the power and impatience to which they testify, and the final signal that unless we admit them freely and fairly into our reckoning, they will break in by the back door of the spirit.

And this for me is the dimension of Rudolf Steiner and his work in general, and in particular that of the Camphill Movement. I myself, alas, have read very little of Steiner. It is not that I minimize his spirit, but solely due to the limits of the capacity of a writer to read more than I have done, quite apart from the awesome task that reading him would be, considering his collected works run to some four hundred volumes. Fortunately, there is a measure more vital than reading, which can convey his substance and significance, and that is through observing the consequences of his being and doing. It is a fact, after all, that one knows more about a human being by his deeds than even by what at his best he can say about himself and his intentions. And I've seen a great deal of what Steiner has contributed to life through the remarkable schools he has inspired all over the world, and his influence on education generally in this life and century.

There is also the influence he has had, not on dogmatic religion, but on the religious climate, his influence on architecture, and raising to new dimensions the spiritual and intellectual dialogue of his day. I myself have experienced gatherings at the Goetheanum which have given all sorts of conditions of intellect and spirit an opportunity to feel they too might contribute somewhat to the re-direction of life, and illumination of our condition. He was a great pioneering, exploring spirit, with a profound, intuitive perception of the necessity of understanding this unease I have mentioned, and leading life into what had been hitherto dark, unfavoured and even forbidden areas of itself. Perhaps one of the most reassuring things about nature and the universe is that whenever their creatures imperil the increase of themselves and creation, they produce the necessary correctives. They do so in the first instance, I believe, by inflicting life with so great a discomfort of spirit that it questions established values and will-ful purposes so deeply as to widen awareness, and so healing and bridging this cleft between light and dark within us.

Should men, however, fail to take up this search for increased awareness and no longer pursue freely a vision of greater totality and wholeness which, as far back as we can go, seems to have been the most sacred of causes to which men can espouse themselves, those terrible healers of plague, disaster and war move in to do it for them.

In the last two hundred years we have had a plentiful mixture of failures of the so-called free and conscious remedies prescribed for the diseases of our inadequacy, as well as those of the terrible healers who terminated the "Age of Reason" and royal rule of the sun in France, with the awful Revolution which is being so strangely celebrated today. The consequences of this one example pursued us in even more horrible revolutions all over the world, of which the revolutions in Russia and China were perhaps the most immediate and substantial imitators. Then in a deceptively peaceful and insidious way, it started to move in with the industrialization of the West, the increasing extroversion and rationalization of the European spirit, the growing materialism, and the severance of man from his instinctive self as he tended to group himself more and more, with vastly increased power over the natural world, in proliferating, sprawling and reeking cities. The cloud over Hiroshima is melodramatic evidence of the awful power and abuse of power brought about by the fevered imagination raised in the course of this comfortable disease.

Yet, as the nineteenth century proceeded, the intimations of the dangers this process was bringing to sanity and well-being, had been perceived in all sorts of intuitive spirits. There is no need to catalogue them all. Every educated person should have his own short list of examples, starting at its most superstitious, for instance with Mme Blavatsky and her Tarot brood, and moving on and up to men like Janet and James and America's most remarkable Mrs Eddy, and all sorts of artists and writers, from Goya and Daumier to poets like Manley Hopkins who is still so strangely underrated and far from popular. But all in their own way sought to warn us of the storm gathering because we would not respond to the needs of our introverted selves and contain this increasing lopsidedness, and rootless extroversion, which was dominating the social scene.

Among the greatest of these intuitives, Steiner was one of the most creative, lucid and valid, to such an extent that what he began stands and remains alive, relevant and dynamic. Nowhere is the re-direction that Steiner's work brought about perhaps more humanly evident than in the work of Camphill. What Camphill does is made specific in the book that follows. I can bear witness to its purpose, the balance and compensation it brings to the deprivation and disproportion of this century which Steiner's spirit so imaginatively confronted. He was always agonizingly aware of how the feeling and caring values so characteristic of the Western spirit at its best, were being destroyed by an arid conversion of lawful reason into a proliferating rationalism and overwhelming preoccupation with material values. As a result what he strove so effectively to bring alive again in human society were precisely these lost and rejected values which had once made it so creative. His inspiration was, in a contemporary way, a profoundly New Testament phenomenon, just as Camphill, to put it the Christian way, is doing New Testament work in a modern idiom, through its care of the despised and rejected, the physically handicapped and the unloved. In doing so, it is characterized by a rediscovery of what are the first and highest values in the natural life of man. Not to abolish what is oldest in man, its work implies, but to make it new and the first, and not the last as it is so often in our hubris of the mind and matter.

I have often been asked what the difference is between so-called civilized man and primitive man. I have always tried to answer by describing what I have experienced of perhaps the oldest form of primitive life: the Bushmen of Africa — Stone Age men who were, as far as we can tell, the first people with whom Western man ever had contact. The difference for me was simple and striking. I found him rich in a way in which we were poor. I found that, above all, he never felt unknown. This haunting sense of being totally unknown that comes to contemporary men and women when they are alone with themselves in the dead hours of the night, was never experienced by the Bushmen. They felt known to everything that surrounded them and hence were full of the sense of all-belonging. Even in their animal stories they would say to me that they ought really to tell me the stories in the language of the lion, or the baboon, or the ostrich, for me to properly understand them, but as I unfortunately did not speak these languages, they would have to tell me about them in their own. The sense of kinship which such sensitivity portrays, presupposes a feeling of being known. It was the feeling out of which St Paul spoke in Corinthians 13, when he acclaimed: "And now I know in part; but then shall I know even as also I am known."

Even the stars knew the first man of the world, and he would say, under a night sky sagging with stars over the desert: "Look, that star is falling because it is on its way to tell others at distant places that one of us has died and that he who was upright has fallen over utterly on to his side. It is on that account that stars fall for us." I remember a night when they began dancing as the full moon rose, and they continued up to a point where even I, who treasured these occasions, felt moved almost to protest and to ask why they went on dancing for so long, and they answered to the effect: "You see that the moon up there is full, and from now on will empty and will start to fade away. It will utterly fade away if we do not show by our dancing how much we want the moon always to be with us, showing men by night with her light the way when the sun has abandoned us."

And I would think, how could human beings possibly be poor, how could they be lost, how could they be full of this dreadful unease, when living longer than men have ever lived before, when materially more secure than men have ever been, with their power over nature and its resources greater than at any time of which we know, and be so possessed by these dreadful feelings of insecurity and helplessness? If only they had still felt as the Bushmen did, that they had the power to influence the phases of the moon and earn the recognition of the stars, I suspect they would never have had so gnawing a sense of meaninglessness. Yet the first men of Africa, however hungry and thirsty and threatened, still found time also to paint, to tell stories, to dance and to laugh in a way in which we cannot laugh today. We know far more today than any primitive man ever did, but we have lost total contact with this feeling of being known, and in the process lost contact with the natural energies for increase which wait out there in the dark of our unknowing, and the reverence for life and meaning which attend them. As a result, there came a loss of reverence for life and an increasing distance between Western man and his own natural self, until all that he feared and hated unconsciously in himself was projected on the first people of southern Africa and he ruthlessly stamped them out to such an extent that today there are very few of the Bushmen left in the vast area of Africa which was once their own.

Nature, which the Victorians held to be "red in tooth and claw" however, had been far kinder to him than our slanted civilization. Both white men and black men — and the black men were by no means primitive men, but, contrary to what people commonly assume, had extremely advanced and sophisticated cultures of their own — combined to destroy the Bushmen without compassion or conscious feelings of doing wrong. It's a story I tell and re-tell, because it's the one true, steady, precise mirror of history in which both black and white in Africa must look and see the reflection of their own fallible human faces, and know how, when they had power over the most natural of men, their uneasy and increasingly insecure and fearful dark selves made them turn on this first spirit of life and extinguish him and his Stone Age civilization. It is the mirror, too, in which our uneasy spirit can stare at the reflection of its guilty and alienated self.

And, of course, the widening of the gulf between modern man and his natural self did not end with this particular abuse of power. Man turned increasingly on the natural world, unchecked and with increasing busy-ness and mad fervour and inventiveness, to exhaust the natural resources of the world and destroy its children, its grass, plants, birds, insects and animals, and poison its water and make the air unbreathable. All these things, Steiner instinctively knew, were part of the failure of our civilization to increase and heighten human awareness, and evidence of the move to narrow and specialize the base of its consciousness, locking out more and more of the redeeming energies which are missing on the threshold of our unconscious spirit. So it is not an accident for me that Camphill and the profound Steiner-induced concern and love it has for the rejected victims of the imperviousness of our age, should have had its own imagination quickened for the first things of the spirit and of life, and found its way like a homing pigeon to Botswana. There, for some years already, it has been working on the fringes of the great wasteland which was the last refuge of the cruelly-persecuted and rejected Bushmen of Africa.

I shall never forget one burning hot day when Jonathan Stedall — with whom I made the first television film about the life of Jung, and other films like *All Africa Within Us* — and I were driving through the southeast corner of Botswana. We were doing a reconnaissance for a film. We intended to go back to the central desert, where I had my own contact with one of the last little groups of Bushmen in the early fifties, to see what more we could do to save him from destruction. The heat was intense, and the country before the rains, desolate and beyond any immediate possibility of growth and increase. It was country I knew well, and it was never flushed with green, except immediately after rare falls of rain. Yet suddenly now, in the wrong season, I saw a vivid streak of green of pocket kerchief measure in that huge, arid surrounding. It reminded Stedall of something I did not know, and he exclaimed: "I have a hunch that could be the new venture Camphill is starting in Botswana."

He was right. I've never forgotten how moved I was to find a small, dedicated mission established in the most primitive conditions but already with facilities to care for the mentally handicapped and physically deformed orphan children of that forgotten world. I remember how affected we both were by the fact that black orphan children and chocolate babies in the care of what looked such a vulnerable and tentative little community seemed already free from fear and confusion. Behind their awkward, contorted movements there was calm and a show of content and hope. I'm not surprised that today an impressive, well-grounded and growing Camphill centre stands there, and numbers of people who have seen it tell me that in those surroundings it is as if a parable were made of flesh and blood.

Accordingly, I feel I cannot do better in describing what I think Camphill and Steiner inspiration are about, than by recalling a great Bushman story which illustrates how, for the Bushman too, in our remotest beginnings, increase of spirit came out of a heightened concern of the imagination for the despised and rejected, accepting them utterly as the material of redemption and transfiguration.

It is the story of how the Bushman's god-hero, the Praying Mantis — Kaggena as they called him in my part of Africa — made the moon. Kaggena, the first and supreme element in Bushman imagination commanding a complex and most meaningful mythology, like all the creators in myth, was of a profoundly paradoxical nature.

One day, he was walking out into the bush on a narrow trail, when he saw a sandal lying discarded by the path. One of the interesting things about the first man of Africa was the fact that he alone of all the indigenous peoples of Africa I knew evolved a sandal for himself: footwear made of good leather, shaped like a foot and with a thong going from between the point where the big toe and its neighbour met in the foot, and being long enough to tie around his ankles like a Greek sandal.

Further, Mantis noticed that this sandal belonged to his eldest son. His eldest son was not even an animal of instinct, but a strange rainbow element, wedded to Porcupine. Porcupine played a wonderful, tender, saving, Ariadne role on the Bushman's desperate labyrinthine way from chaos and old night, through all the challenges of the greatest natural world there has ever been, and onwards until the moment where the Bushman was contained in a deeply-rooted and evolving culture. Here, already, one has to accept that the first man was not literal but spoke in symbols, and one of his greatest symbols was this firstborn son of Mantis, and his incor poration in the rare rainbow element of the desert sky.

The rainbow, of course, is one of the oldest symbols of the discriminating, selective and analytical consciousness of man. It is so in the story of the Flood. It is fitting, therefore, that this spirit should not go barefoot but be sandalled, and that the sandal should become an image of the chosen, consciously-fashioned way the first man took through his world.

Discarded alongside a trail in the bush, the sandal represented something which the conscious spirit of Mantis's future self, the firstborn, had rejected. Mantis pounces on the sandal, and he takes it to a deep pool in the bush where there are reeds and rushes bent low with bird's nests over the water, and bees humming and butterflies on slow wings, and the song of warblers and desert thrushes and the dove they called "po-pori" resounding all around. It is a place which recurs again and again, as wells do in the Pentateuch stories wherever significant things and meetings of man and providence have to take place. Mantis leaves the sandal in the pool and goes back to his shelter chanting his happiness as he goes. For three days at dawn, he is at the pool and he watches the sandal transforming deep at the heart of this image of the profound, mysterious area of the collective unconscious which has the gift of new life in its keeping. His heart quickens, and already at the second dawn he sees there is a tiny antelope called Eland coming alive. On the third day he has no doubts that the metamorphosis is almost complete.

On the fourth, he is there even earlier, and finds standing by this pool, flushed with dawn, a young eland calf, trembling and unsteady on its legs. Singing to himself, he proceeds to rub the wet off the eland, and for three days attends it and rubs it all over with wild honey, the honey whose sweetness is not only an image of natural love, but also of the wisdom, the patience, the industry, and the infinite sum of minute care and ultimate reward that is reflected in the culture which the bee serves. At last, Mantis sings a song which praises the qualities that are incorporated in this beautiful animal, so great now that when the eland walks, the earth around him resounds.

But, unknown to Mantis some of his brothers have been watching, and when Mantis is gone they take the animal and slaughter it so there is nothing left of it but the gall. This outcome may sound cruel, but it is part of the symbolic orchestration of the process of metamorphosis. Mantis's people believed that as you ate, so you became, so that this killing and eating is a remote archaic enactment of a kind of Eucharist, implying that it is only by this eating of what Mantis has created that they themselves can become part of the creation Mantis intended.

Mantis, meanwhile, at the end of a long day of work — he was always busy at something — coming by the pool sees what has happened and is deeply distressed. He is distressed not so much at the killing and consumption of his creation, but by the fact that he was not allowed to take part in it, and he is experiencing both the tragedy, the affirmation, and the glory of all creators faced with the spectacle of their creation. All are instruments, as well as victims of love, and its demands on the overall creator. Like Moses, he can lead others to a land of promise but cannot enter himself. He has to accept that the creator is subject to the law of his own creation, and that in creation, the created must be separate and distanced from its creator if the power to create beyond itself is to be lost.

He acts out a paradox of what has happened, in a fierce argument with the gall. The gall was always the one part of the animal that primitive man could not eat or use, and it represents all that is bitter, unstomachable and indigestible in tragedy. He tells the gall that he is going to jump on it and pierce it so that it is dispersed. The gall says that if you dare do that to me, I will cover you all over with black so that you are blind and cannot see. And this, of course, is precisely the danger of the tragedy, that it hurts and blinds so the victim cannot see its way. The argument between the two rages until, at last, Mantis is driven to discover his ultimate courage, and jumps on the gall and pierces it. The gall explodes and covers, as it said it would, his head and eyes with black, and Mantis is left grovelling on the ground looking for something with which he can wipe the dark from his eyes. He grovels until it seems that he is at the moment of accepting failure, when his left hand suddenly feels something soft and strange at the tip of its fingers. He feels further and a great surge of hope goes through him. It is the feather of an ostrich, a feather of the Promethean bird from whom he, Mantis, had stolen fire and given man consciousness. With this feather he wipes all the gall from his eyes, stands up straight again, balances the feather between both hands and then tosses it up into the air, telling it that it must henceforth be the moon, to bring light in the dark where there had been no light before, and that by this shining to enable men to find their way home in the dark when the great sun they knew so well had abandoned them.

The moon, as another great Bushman story tells us, is a symbol of love and compassion, and evidence of something in life that would let men know how in dying they, like the moon in dying, are renewed again. It is a symbol of all the feeling and the caring values that we are losing in this moment of technological barbarism and abuse of our own power over other men and their societies, and above all, the earth and its children.

Some of the greatest Zen spirits, who had such a remarkable influence on the evolution of the Japanese, and still have to this day, not only for Japan but other cultures as well, talked of the need for man to have a moon heart-mind. I myself, in the 1950s, at the end of a long account of Mantis and his doings, wrote and warned that we lived in a sunset hour of time, and that we no longer needed the sunlike light of reason that has brought us so much, but the light of the moon, all the intuitive and caring values and above all the compassion it represented for man in the past. I added that it was as if I heard on a wind of evening the voice of Mantis calling from an age of stone to an age of men with hearts of stone: "You must be the moon, and you must gently shine in the dark to show men the way when the light of the sun has gone."

I have no doubt that Camphill is an expression of a great intuitive thrust out of the deep heart of nature which has us in its keeping, and knows that both we and it are in mortal peril, urging us to look deeply again into what we have so casually and comfortably tossed aside as if it were nothing but an outworn sandal. Already, in my travels around the world, I am meeting more and more people who think they are alone and lonely. It is true that they are alone — as all men must be if they are to grow into themselves — but the loneliness is unnecessary, because the world contains so many close neighbours, who no longer live next door, the closest often the furthest away. More and more people are appearing every day, who belong to a community which is still to come. They have no establishment as yet to express what they seek, yet there are these pilot schemes of the world to come, like Camphill and the schools associated with it, so that there is no excuse for not beginning to know, as the first man knew when he looked and gathered his imagination around his moon, that, Hamlet-wise, "there is a special providence in the fall of a sparrow . . . if it be not now, yet it will come: the readiness is all."

And this venture from a lost world beyond its fringes tells us that readiness is coming, that although separate and alone — to use a word induced in me by Dante's *Paradiso* — men are about to be "neighboured" again, and that the moon-heart is on its way.

Introduction

Cornelius M. Pietzner

The evolution of this book about communities — the Camphill Communities — was itself very much a reflection of a community process. The complement of contributors, the stylistic diversity, the scope of different voices, and, too, the encumbrances which come with many voices, were also present. This is not a book so much *about* the Camphill Movement as *of* the Camphill Movement. In its own way it is a reflection of community. Some of these elements continually evolve and change and if this book had been composed a year earlier or a year hence no doubt it would be very different.

Perhaps one could look at this chronicle not only as text and photographs, but also as intention and as experiment. There is no single author, nor even group, but a speckled collage of contributors, most of whose professions lie in the tantalizingly "unprofessional" arena of social life, of community building, of social art, of living life together. Our writers are senior Camphill co-workers, new participants, handicapped people, board and council members, parents, brothers, sisters, friends, old and young. Some are able to formulate their thoughts more traditionally than others. Some sing their song unrestrained and freely, yet all have something to offer. We have not altered or co-ordinated stylistic idiosyncrasies to "smooth" things out. The differences offer texture and tonality to the larger pattern of these pages.

This publication is an attempt at self-expression. Obviously the key question focuses on what individual or collective "self" is being imparted. How does even a single community, working together with individuals, some of whom are vulnerable or handicapped, express itself? How does a tightly knit spiritual community "collective" coherently express itself if it includes nearly 8,000 people, many more people indirectly, and spans oceans, continents, cultures and traditions, laws and regulations?

This collective or family of communities we call the Camphill Movement. This term has evolved quite naturally and is used less to connote a grassroots sectarian "movement", than to indicate a far-flung nexus of deeply connected individuals and communities who both retain their independence and recognize their interdependence.

Perhaps this interdependence, reliant so heavily on both inner and outer mobility, is one of the reasons why we have chosen not to ask an "elder" to articulate the Camphill Movement on our behalf, or a friendly observer to harmonize our song and correct our grammar. Rather, we encourage many to speak, many to sing. Some offer a line, and others a verse or refrain.

This is a risk, of course, and we have employed the powerful component of photographic images to weld and harmonize much of what this book is trying to convey. The reader will understand the challenge of imparting fundamental aspects through any single medium about a community structure such as Camphill. Deference, therefore, is given to the outer, observable characteristics. Yet even these are almost beyond reach as the differences extant in the communities of Camphill are great. Camphill in Botswana is different from Camphill in Switzerland or Norway or America. How then, if Camphill is so disparate, does the common community component articulate itself? Is Camphill simply a conglomerate of individual communities, each one entirely independent and unrelated to the next, or are there deeper, more profound connections that link the Camphill Movement as an identifiable spiritual and life-community?

Certainly there is collectivization, actually at every level of the community. Why else would we call ourselves a Community, and more importantly, feel connected to each other, even when some live in Africa, some in Norway, some in America? The great power of the individual spirit is *not* lost or subsumed to some communal "way". Rather it is because of the increasing development and realization of the individual spirit that community is so relevant, even urgent, in these times.

On the one hand we experience an ever greater stridency in personal opinion, in individuation, in the isolation of the self (so prevalent in urban concentrations), the difficulty in accepting the "other". "Each man an island" becomes normative, and recognition of our fundamental commonality is narrowed into ethnic and nationalistic expressions.

On the other side the negation of the individual spirit is widely experienced in western culture. One need not look far to discover evidence of this. The economics of mass production have infiltrated cultural life to saturation point. Indeed, political apathy, social isolation, alienation, cultural impoverishment, educational breakdown — the list could go on — have battered and bruised the vitality of the individual spirit. Community life can be a very potent antidote to this phenomenon, calling on the creative engagement of the individual in a fundamental, stimulating and direct way.

It was most likely unimaginable in 1938 that Camphill, then a hardly formulated vision burning in a few young people, and carried by the powerful personality of Karl König, would be asked to grow to the extent it has. The beginnings were more than modest; they were outwardly meagre. Yet they also represented a true commitment to a social ideal, fashioned out of the ravages of the Second World War. Chapter 2 of this book describes the development of Camphill into well over seventy interdependent communities around the world. Each community has its own core of co-workers, its trainees/seminarists in adult education courses, its own parents' and friends' circles, its own governing group or body, its own ever-expanding circles of "professionals" and individuals connected to the work in some way or another. Everybody has a part to play, a contribution to make, and when the Camphill Movement is referred to, it must actually include all these people!

Camphill has not only grown outwardly over the last fifty years, it has metamorphosed inwardly as well. This inward growth, so stimulating, so frustrating, so immense, is the reason that a definitive description of Camphill would be limiting and inaccurate. The spirit of a child, a group, or a community such as Camphill, is at once obvious and elusive. To try and contain it through a static definition would be simplistic.

I hope this lack of definition stimulates questions in place of answers, as questions tend to liberate and ready answers restrict. It is not a ploy, editorial or otherwise, to avoid definition or imply limitations. This book will be justified if it leaves the reader hungry or even curious to find out more about this enigma called Camphill.

If you would ask every person who has written something about Camphill in these pages: "What is Camphill?" you might hear as many different answers. "It is a place for peace, born out of the struggle of living together as a community." "It is a cultural commitment, an island in the sea of impoverishment." "A place where the sanctity of earth — land and animals — of people of different orientations, can be invested with meaning, with respect, with devotion." "It is a way of life that calls upon us to face each other, to face ourselves, to hold ourselves accountable for what we do and for *how* we do it."

The idea of healing or therapeutic communities can be applied in its broadest sense to Camphill. Certainly Camphill has been "recognized" for its work with developmentally disabled people. It has won awards, been written about in news media, professional journals, been lauded by agencies, dignitaries and various officials for this work. Yet over the course of time Camphill has also turned to elderly people in its care, to the questions of youth, to urban blight and deprivation, to juvenile delinquents and socially maladjusted young people. This is quite broad in itself, but we must widen the concept even further. We must look at *ourselves* — no longer as the helper, teacher or therapist, but as the helped, the taught, the receiver.

There is not one "class" of healers and another to be healed. Evermore we *all* participate and suffer in the inadequacy and nakedness of our single selves; and we all receive. This is a fundamental tenet of the social-therapeutic work of Camphill. The surrender of fixed ideas — of who provides care to whom — has become an experience borne out of decades of social encounter, therapeutic encounter, community encounter, human encounter.

Such an orientation is predicated on the recognition of the eternal in each one of us, handicapped or less handicapped. It assumes an inviolate spiritual entelechy in each person, and presents disability, and ability, in a different context than what we are perhaps accustomed to. Increasingly, one can speak about these things, and they no longer stun or startle us. It is as if slowly the higher powers of perception of the individual recognize the truth of their own existence, and one has the possibility, the mandate even, to invest each other with renewed meaning.

These things are important to Camphill, and are written about further on. Quite suddenly, we find ourselves in new landscapes; no longer in "service communities" for disabled people, but in settings of discovery, challenge, growth, metamorphosis in which *people* are important, and classifications or typologies become transformed and lose meaning in a traditional sense.

There is something almost inexorable about Camphill's outer aspects. Yet behind this growth lies a fragility which I can only relate to the challenge to the individual spirit. This is a challenge to review one's sense of humanity, to modify one's sense of self, to enhance one's sense of the other, of another's potential, another's gifts. Unfortunately, not all attitudes are frail, but often those which call on our sense of wonderment and awe, our devotion and care for the small things, need support and effort again and again. While the individual spirit consciousness is strong, at times even invincible, its willingness to work upon *itself*, if I may put it in this way, is tender. I *am* responsible for my attitudes and their care and cultivation. My attitudes represent themselves clearly in the ongoing social fabric of a community, in this instance the Camphill Community. Indeed, this is so for all of us who live in community and makes the community both dependent on and vulnerable to the individual. The community requires the individual just as the individual needs the community. Indeed, the lens of community brings into sharp focus the emphasis on individual responsibility, perhaps as a modern-day paradox.

This book is not meant as a testament to outer achievement or growth. It could be a reminder (of which there are many others) of different ways, of alternatives, of the individual process of *becoming*, not only of *what is*. Perhaps it is a reminder of the force of the creative spirit that brings man together with his fellow man in his search for himself, and his search for the Godhead. The new community will play an ever stronger part in this quest.

This book was essentially the idea of Anke Weihs, a founding member of Camphill. Her brilliance could have fashioned a more precise articulation of Camphill than almost anybody. In the early stages of this book, Anke crossed the threshold of death, yet her involvement has been felt throughout. Thus, the dedication to Anke is sufficiently natural as to also include all the hundreds, the thousands, who have given and taken as part of this "festival", this "folk-dance" called the Camphill Movement.

The documentary aspect of this book is clear, yet it is not entirely retrospective. The middle of the book is the "heart region" and pulses toward the future. Chapter 3 has no photographs. It contains personal accounts yet these are the ones that also point towards the future. They belong to this more tender part of Camphill. They belong to this invincible part of Camphill.

The other chapters, both in the beginning and toward the end, lead up to the present from the beginnings of Camphill. Our past is formative indeed, and it must be so. It gives direction, and orientation, a resolve. However, it is not absolute, and here and there one sees Camphill veering off, turning where one might not have expected it, adding an element, refining a concentration, taking a new step. (This is not dissimilar to other biographies imbued as they are with elements of a divine artistry, which we decry as unpredictability or fate!)

A life story is more easily recognizable in retrospect than in the forecast of the future. Camphill's future is neither fixed nor settled. There is form, there is substance, there is history — at least half a century of it — not including all its antecedents. There is a context for Camphill but to assume that the future is either guaranteed or predictable would be not to understand the difference between a prototype or model and a creative force, an impulse, an idea, a vision.

Cornelius Pietzner
Camphill Soltane, United States

Acknowledgements

There are too many who helped with this book to thank by name. However, Nora and Friedwart Bock carried a great deal of work throughout. Also to be mentioned are Nick Poole in England, and Jonathan Stedall of the BBC who made it possible to share Camphill with Laurens van der Post. Particular and also personal thanks to Sir Laurens, whose willingness to participate in this book despite an incredible workload seems to confirm that harmony which so many of us have felt with his great work.

I am also indebted to my co-workers in Camphill Soltane, and in particular my wife Elisabeth, whose forbearance and support allowed me the necessary hours at odd and often inconvenient times to put this book together.

Chapter 1

Karl König — a portrait

Christof-Andreas Lindenberg

Karl König's life between 1939 and 1966 and the unfolding and growth of Camphill is so linked as to be one story. To relate this part of his biography is also to find the manifestation of an impulse that led to a world-wide movement of homes, schools and villages on four continents. The thought that König was solely responsible for the development of Camphill must be balanced by the very core of the impulse: the idea of community. Thus the story of the founder group of young people who gathered around the Königs in Vienna from 1936 to 1938 is an integral part.

Interrupted in their studies by the annexation of Austria by Nazi Germany, many of the group gathered again with the Königs in a small manse in north-east Scotland just before the Second World War to work together for an ideal. Then there is the story of those who joined the founding group after the war, and of the many who came to live and work with the growing Camphill Movement as part of their unfolding destinies. Community building is the inherent force in this growth process which involves many people, not just one man. This introduction gives a picture of one man's unique contribution to Camphill, and its growth in seventeen countries. The development of the seventy-four Camphill centres is due to all, handicapped or not, who form the living communities. Karl König, however, is rightly referred to as the founder of the Camphill Movement.

Small in stature but great in bearing, Karl König was a controversial figure. How was he experienced? Many instances come to mind. As always for his lectures, the Camphill Hall is filled to capacity. Dr König steps forward, a folder held tightly under his left arm. He walks with customary deliberation to the table. Then he rearranges his space: the glass of water, the flowers, sometimes the position of the table is altered, if only a little, no matter how carefully some of the "old hands" have prepared everything. Having arranged his books, he clasps his hands behind his back, straightens up as if in a moment of decision, fastens his gaze on a point above the audience, and begins, often in a kind of questioning tone. "Dear friends, I have the impression that it would be necessary for us to turn to the coming Easter festival . . ." His voice does not dwell on addressing the audience. There is almost no break between "Dear friends" and what follows, which has the effect of taking the listeners right into the question of the coming seasonal festival. König lived strongly with the signs of the times. In lectures, his audience often had the impression that he read these signs from a place behind them, and, as his gaze indicated, a little above their heads. By beginning his talks in this way, Dr König could free us from our narrow questioning and we would often find ourselves conversing in the present tense with the spirit of the occasion.

He shunned figures of speech or intellectual excursions. He was very direct. Often quoting Rudolf Steiner verbatim, he linked these passages with our situation. Steiner's words became contemporary through König. He demanded our attention and his eyes would flash if somebody interrupted him with a cough, or nodded off to sleep. König was a master at creating imagery that helped us follow his line of thought. He once described the seasons of the year in their outgoing movement from winter to summer, adding the image of arterial blood streaming from the heart to the capillaries. And he compared the descending, centring half of the year toward

20

Christmas to the venous blood returning to the heart. He spoke of the possibility of threshold experiences when going from one half of the year to the other, and the kinds of mental illness which may arise: the schizophrenic tendency in entering the ascending part of the year; the manic-depressive tendency on crossing from the height of summer to the depth of winter. Such images often helped us to deepen our grasp of the concept.

He was also adept at imitating the animals he described, so we had the impression that he actually became the sparrow, or squirrel he was talking about. A zoologist at heart, he deemed it a privilege when the opportunity arose to turn to the animal world. He delighted his listeners. Whether in a light or grave mood, most of his talks addressed themselves to our potential to become more awake, useful and essential in our anthroposophical striving. His public talks never failed to inspire moral enthusiasm, often changing people's lives there and then. The person of König and the spoken word were synonymous.

When I think of Karl König the writer, I remember the concentration of his posture, the deliberate way he held his big fountain pen, how his arms bent in an action of utmost intensity. I know that I witnessed a man of will. Through his writing he was in touch with the whole world: he prepared the founding of centres, he startled the experts with his medical papers, he comforted parents and taught out of his knowledge of Anthroposophy. One of König's close friends told me how he had managed to get so many people to help with the Camphill Movement: "He always answered their letter of inquiry quickly." Indeed, a look at his desk showed that he always seemed to be up to date. To anyone visiting him this was a marvel. To those of us who knew the number of letters and papers he dealt with daily it was beyond comprehension how he accomplished the work.

As early as 1942, when the first Down's syndrome children came to Camphill, König had researched the disease with profound interest. He loved these children and so he pondered the riddle that they pose. Seventeen years later he published the first clinical study to appear in German.* Like other pioneers in curative education before him, the enigmas encountered stirred the doctor and humanitarian in him to put questions and investigate ways of helping and healing these children. With new insights, he regularly wrote about the spastic, the thalidomide sufferer, and the disturbed conditions he met in the thousands of children that came to him. Apart from itinerant consultations, he had the experience of many children in the community setting of the Camphill schools. By holding conferences with resident or visiting doctors, and working with those who looked after the children, he formulated treatment and educational methods. He fostered meetings where this spirit of inquiry could be shared. This fulfils an unwritten law of community life: one's own question gains in the same measure by which it is recognized to live in others. I believe that König wrote all his books out of such a recognition, and so the books are not his creations alone. This is true not only for the study in child psychology, on the order of birth in the family, which was published as *Brothers and Sisters*, when almost every co-worker helped by supplying data, but also for *The Human Soul*, and perhaps his most outstanding book, *The First Three Years of the Child*. His insights were "ploughed under", as it were, in seminars, and worked through in a supplementary way by the experiences of others; always linking his creative thought with living reality.

Karl König documented his wide-ranging interests in hundreds of articles that stretched from his major interest, embryology, to history, human biography, and zoology. Many things were written by the medical doctor, by the teacher, and by the research scientist. He also wrote what one could call petitions for the social standing of the handicapped. Other writings were prompted by his ever-growing concern for the suffering of man and the needs of the earth. The attack on the dignity and integrity of man called him to write and speak. He often wrote long scripts for his lectures, complete with quotations. When giving the same talk in another place, or in a slightly different context, he wrote it out again with a seemingly untiring pen. Here

Opposite: Karl König, founder of the Camphill movement.

* *Der Mongolismus.*

21

Dr König with a Down's syndrome child.

was a man who always managed to link his active thought-life with the will to write.

In contrast stands the artist writer. In quieter moments, or when he was ill, Karl König created poems or lyric stories. Friends put together a volume for his sixtieth birthday which, understandably, leaves out the more personal selection. Among his best works are the festival plays which, still, bring the community together in a special way in the season of the year they highlight. König always had a particular cast in mind when writing these dramas, but the plays have been performed successfully by other groups. Some of the plays are more like pageants, involving the whole gathering of people. The most well-known is the St John's play, for midsummer. In it, the players gradually form into a bell, singing, swinging and intertwining; the bell of mankind. The players end in a reconciling circle of oneness. No words can bring close the experience of an unfolding community as do such celebrations enacted in harmony, when the word is lifted to common movement and song.

In September 1952, at his fiftieth birthday celebration in Camphill House, Karl König agreed to play a piano duet with Susi Lissau; a rare pleasure for us. Then he told us that he had never felt that he had aged. As a child and throughout his youth, he always felt himself to be the same unchangeable self. While he assumed this to be a common experience, we realized that it was perhaps more true for him than for others. A photograph from 1927 shows the young man of twenty-five with the expression of someone in their late forties; deep wrinkles and a moustache complete the impression. Already as a child he had a wise, knowing look in his eye.

Karli, as his Jewish mother called him, was born on Thursday, September 25, 1902, to parents who owned a shoe shop in Vienna. In that year the Swedish educationist Ellen Key proclaimed the twentieth century as the Century of the Child. Well loved and cared for, he nevertheless did not have an easy childhood. Being an only child, born with slightly crippled feet and over-awake in his senses and soul, he looked into the world precociously. There was something special about the child. When the two-year-old blond curly-head sat in his push-chair outside the shoe shop, a psychology professor, strolling by, was startled enough to go into the shop and inquire to whom the child belonged. He told the proud mother: "He will be a very famous man in later life. In my whole career of studying heads I never came across so special a form as this child's head."

The growing child did not mix much with other children, but helped his parents in the shoe shop. Once he said: "School-time was not altogether smooth-running." The parents witnessed with concern an all too early independence. They found a picture of Christ in his cupboard when he was eleven years old. Although he celebrated the customary Jewish bar mitzvah at the age of thirteen, he had already begun to find his own way to Christianity.

His social awareness at the beginning of the First World War made him a young St Martin, sharing his cloak with the beggars he saw around him. He refused to eat his mother's home baking when he thought others were starving. The growing boy spoke out when he witnessed cruelty to animals, and was arrested by the police for doing so. König described himself as self-willed. There were the increasing migraine attacks. As the youth grew up, his mother noted: "There was such sadness in him, as though he had to carry the whole pain of the world alone." His eyes saw, his ears listened to the dilemma of his time, long before he was a grown man and could do something about it.

Towards the end of his schooling, Karli was deeply immersed in Haeckel, Freud, Buddha and Lao-tzu, Dumas and Balzac, but especially the New Testament, seeking his way. His library grew when, after a quiet and successful matriculation, the eighteen-year-old youth studied all the necessary texts for natural scientific research with, he said, "a primeval force" that came over him. He was then in his pre-medical year. When he was finally led to Goethe's natural scientific writings, he compared his enlightenment with what he had experienced when he had found the New Testament. In 1921 he heard of Rudolf Steiner, and found a group of doctors and students who were discussing Steiner's lectures on the study of man. Then came the important discovery on reading Steiner's *Philosophy of Spiritual Activity:* "Here is all I myself have noted down on nature's creative force in human thinking." It was an overwhelming experience. He wanted to meet Steiner, but missed going to his East-West Congress in Vienna in June 1922. He never had another opportunity for the much wished-for encounter.

König the medical student was also a teacher and research worker. For three years he worked at the Embryological Institute of Vienna, and while there, at the age of twenty-three, he published his first research papers. When König graduated in 1927, Alfred Fischel, dean of the university, wished to employ him as an assistant at the Embryological Institute, as long as he would keep Anthroposophy to himself, a condition that decided Dr König to decline the offer. He had become a member of the Anthroposophical Society and would follow a different calling. In the summer of 1927, Dr König gave his first lecture at a public anthroposophical conference. He then worked for some months in a children's hospital, his name rapidly becoming known. And then the call came.

Dr Ita Wegman, leader of the medical section of the Steiner-instituted School of Spiritual Science in Dornach, Switzerland, came to Vienna on a brief visit. Meeting Dr König briefly, she invited him to work at her Clinical Therapeutic Institute in Arlesheim, near Dornach. He accepted at once.

In the weeks that followed, destiny played a significant part. Entering the clinic, he met his future wife, the nurse Tilla Maasberg, who had arrived from Silesia that same November day.

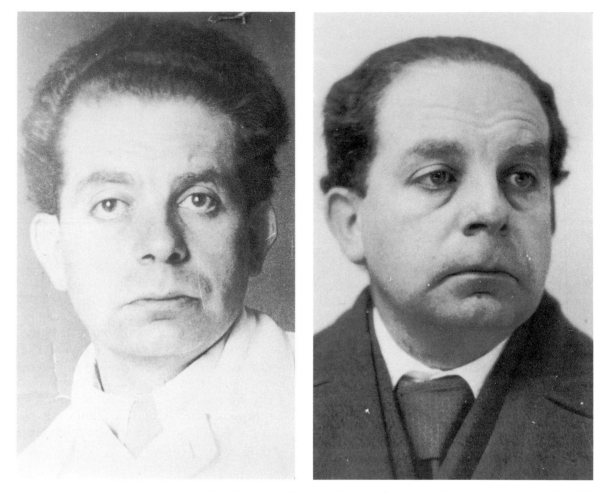

Twenty days later, on Advent Sunday, he witnessed the Advent garden and saw very handicapped children walking with lighted candles in a very special festival. He wrote afterward: "In this hour the decision was taken that I would dedicate my life to the care and education of these children. It was a promise I gave to myself: to build a hill upon which a big candle was to burn so that many infirm and handicapped children would be able to find their way to this beacon of hope and to light their own candles so that each single flame would be able to radiate and shine forth." In the clinic he could deepen the anthroposophical approach to medicine. This work was reflected in a series of articles on embryology, then the foremost subject on his mind. König the writer had emerged.

A little more than four weeks after the Advent experience in the Sonnenhof, König was encouraged by Dr Wegman to hold his first lecture in the makeshift hall of the Goetheanum at Dornach during the Christmas Conference. He spoke on world evolution as reflected in embryological stages of development, based on his recent studies. This successful talk heralded the arrival of König the lecturer and led to a lecture tour to Breslau. This tour was to lead him to the place of his future work. For the next seven years, Karl and Tilla König put all their efforts into the new curative home, Pilgramshain, in Silesia, working with handicapped children. Destiny had spoken, and a life of dedication to the child in need of special care, and to the handicapped person in need of integration, had been born out of those portentous weeks in Switzerland.

Dorothea von Jeetze, now in her nineties and living in Camphill Village Copake in America, recalls how Dr König came to Pilgramshain. She tells how he visited a small children's home run by the Maasberg sisters while on his lecture tour. On Ascension day in mid-May, he was seriously asked to work there, but could not imagine practising in such a small place. The same day, Joachim and Dorothea von Jeetze came seeking acceptance of their offer of their nearby mansion house and park at Pilgramshain for the Maasbergs' and A. Strohscheins' curative education work. Now König felt doubly attracted, for he was already very connected to Tilla Maasberg and to her Herrenhut (Moravian Brethren) background, and now there was also the offer of a castle and grounds. Great moments call for quick decisions. The curative home in Pilgramshain was started that August, and in September Dr König joined the venture. He married Tilla the following year. As well as acting as doctor for the home, he also built up a medical practice in the area which, in the next seven years, was to draw a large number of patients. The requests for lectures also increased.

Little is written about the years at Pilgramshain, but it is clear that there König developed his medical approach to mental retardation and organizational insight to residential care. What had to wait for another time was the concept of community, both from a social and spiritual standpoint. Dr König was thirty-three when, under political pressure and impelled to search further, he decided to leave Germany. He could not take any money over the border into Austria, and he arrived back in his home town to what appeared to be a new beginning. It turned out to be different.

The two year period he spent in Vienna was a time of inner and outer preparation. The group of young people who gathered around the busy doctor were to become lifelong friends and co-founders, and their enthusiasm was kindled by Dr König's weekly talks and their discussions. Many of them had Jewish backgrounds and they soon felt the pressure of Nazi Germany. On the day of Austria's annexation to Germany, March 11, 1938, they were ready to disperse, but remained bound to each other. That day remains as a kind of eleventh hour for the whole of Europe. The world does not need strategy and outer actions, the future depends on silent deeds performed in mutual recognition, and a minute little band of people left home and country to do that. They were to kindle a community fire which now burns in many countries, and in many hearts.

Dr König could be a difficult person to approach. Yet every time, on entering his room, one was at once reassured by his welcome. He seemed to know you, and in the brief time allotted, mostly half an hour, unspoken doubts were dispelled and superficial analyses of a situation corrected. Meeting him, one felt warmer. This must have been the experience of the many thousands of people who sought his counsel, whether in a personal meeting or by writing to him; the meeting of warmth through being recognized. We often witnessed it when he spoke to children; a bridge of warmth was created in that moment. Dr König always had a lot of things on his mind. In the course of a day he would meet very many destiny stories, some disturbing matters, be faced with a variety of difficult situations, while having to plan lectures, courses, journeys and confirm the work and direction in the new places. However, in a private meeting you always met his undivided attention and love. The accompanying challenge to do better was not the main thing you took away, but rather the thought that you had untapped resources for doing infinitely better; an enthusiasm and confidence engendered by the increased flowing warmth. A phenomenon of the Camphill Movement is the uninterrupted growth in the number of people coming to join the work. Dr König had the rare gift of knowing almost all the many co-workers by name. He knew the people who supported the work, the parents, and so very many special children and villagers; and in turn all felt known by this man of the heart. His unbounded human interest penetrated the whole movement. And he always included those who had died.

Near the end of his life, Karl König wrote:

Only the help from man to man — the encounter of Ego with Ego — the becoming aware of the other man's individuality without enquiring into his creed, world conception or political affiliations, but simply the meeting, eye to eye, of two persons creates that curative education which counters, in a healing way, the threat to our innermost humanity. This, however, can only be effective if with it a fundamental recognition is taken into consideration, a recognition which has to come out of the heart.*

It is difficult to imagine the change from Vienna city life to that in a remote granite manse in the north-east of Scotland; out in the windblown countryside, without amenities or electric light. From March 30, 1939, the growing group of Austrian refugees learnt, day by day, to handle broom and hoe and create a home for twelve children in need of special care. Thirteen months later, the men in the group were interned as enemy aliens. During their six-month absence, the women brought about the birth of Camphill. On June 1, 1940, the move into Camphill House and estate near Aberdeen took place. The way that led from the humblest of beginnings to that spiritually determined beginning is what makes that day a true birthday, and justifies using the name Camphill to cover the whole world-wide movement.

When he was applying for planning permission, Karl König wrote down as the purpose of the intended work: medical, curative-educational and agricultural pursuits. That gave freedom for future development. Long before the Camphill villages came into being, Dr König, Thomas Weihs and others had deepened their knowledge of biodynamic agriculture. König arranged medical conferences for doctors, nurses and therapists, and with the many helping physicians laid a foundation for the gradual development of a science of curative education. This is taught in the International Camphill Seminar held in many countries.

Dr König became ill in 1955. Recovering, he entered the most intense period of involvement in the expanding Camphill Movement. During his last eleven years he was able to help in the threefold ordering of life within the centres, as well as establishing villages and schools in Germany, the United States, Switzerland, Ireland, Holland and Scandinavia. His heart was world-wide, but his focus and will were directed to the immediate surroundings. A fine example of his greatness was his ability to delegate and foster responsibility for the impulse and all realms of work. He gave up his chairmanship of the Camphill Movement, acting as *primus inter pares*. From the beginning, the Camphill work was built, formed and carried by many people. At the end of his life the king in him had fully united with the shepherd. In 1965 he said again that the handicapped children and adults are our true teachers, and that he too was learning daily from the life together with them.

I have tried to sketch the man of imaginative thought, the man of determined will, and the man of great heart to paint a portrait of a unique brother for those in need. Only by surveying the whole development and present position of the Camphill Movement can Karl König's contribution be rightly estimated. Other articles and pictures in this book give a view of the diversity of the work. But it stands out clearly that one man in particular was able to bring down the right thoughts and perform the necessary deeds at the right moment. Thus Karl König, in the years from 1939 until his death on March 27, 1966, was the ongoing founder of the world-wide Camphill Movement indeed.

* *Camphill Brief*,
Christmas 1965.

Camphill essentials

Karl König

> We men of the present age
> Are in need of the right ear
> For the Spirit's morning call
> St Michael's morning call.
> Knowledge of the spiritual world
> Will open the portals of the soul
> Towards true hearing of this morning call.

(Verse by Rudolf Steiner spoken at the beginning of every College meeting.)

Dr König repeatedly felt urged to put his experiences into imaginatively formulated thoughts that became spiritual nourishment for others. The following introduction to an essay was written for the Cresset, a Camphill journal, at Christmas 1959. It allows the reader to sense how individual destiny can be woven into the destiny of the community, and from there become part of the tapestry of the destiny of mankind through "the right ear for the Spirit's morning call".

The Camphill Movement

Christmas 1959 — and it is twenty one years ago that I first celebrated this festival here in Britain and not in my own country. I was sitting in a tiny room, in one of the hundreds of back streets of London. Alone, a drop in the vast human sea of a city, a stranger, a foreigner. I knew that with me, tens of thousands of people shared the same fate. Men and women, old and young, children and adults, we were all in the same boat. It was the boat of loneliness; a ship without a destination, a life uprooted from the native soil and barely saved, like a plant which is given a handful of earth in a little pot of clay. How shall we survive?

The small candle in front of me lit the few green branches on the mantlepiece and the gas fire hummed a low song. My thoughts went out into the future. Will it be possible to turn this lonely life into order and shape again? Will the fragments of my existence be put together again so that they may build a new frame? I was one of the many who were just too young to be a soldier in the First World War. Then came a time of breathtaking recovery and all seemed to be well when, gradually, a second war appeared on the horizon. And here I was, thrown out of my work and I felt like one who, after a shipwreck, was cast on to a lonely, unknown island.

The flame of the candle jerked and quivered and threw strange shadows on the wall. I had left Europe behind me. Here it was no more the land of Europe; it was a country of the Western World. The language was foreign to me; the people were strangers. Their way of living was not my way and their past was almost unknown to me. I had a different background, different modes of existence, different thoughts. Some of these strangers had turned to me with a friendly gesture. Others, on whom I had previously counted, showed no more interest than just the limits of good behaviour would permit.

I was alone! Will I again have the strength to begin anew? In a few days my wife and children were to arrive and, in several countries on the Continent, a number of young friends were waiting to join me. Join me in what? Will I be permitted to work? And if so, what kind of work was I to do? But in Italy and France, in Holland and Switzerland, in Germany and Czechoslovakia, friends were waiting to join me! A house had been found in the north of Scotland where we could start to live together. But what kind of life will we live? It will become only an enclave in this land; we will be strangers in a big community. And what is our task?

The light of the candle now was quiet and bright and my eyes turned to a small book which a kind person had given me as a Christmas present. It was an English Bible; never before had I held one in my hands. I was astonished to realize that the present translation was sponsored by James I, a man and monarch for whom, for many years, I had had the highest esteem. I had learnt to admire this "greatest fool of Christendom" and I read now the following words in the dedication: ". . . to go forward with the confidence and resolution of a man maintaining the truth of Christ, and propagating it far and near . . ." Is this not common ground on which I may stand, I asked myself.

It was common ground. And now I saw and knew some more about the future task which

Below left: Dr König with Lic. Emil Bock (left).

lay before me. I saw Austria overrun and conquered by men who had betrayed the very essence of Europe. They had turned it into a camp of nationalists, searching for might and power. Europe was overcome by their vain glory and was preparing to become a battlefield. Could we not take a morsel of the true European destiny and make it into a seed so that some of its real task may be preserved? A piece of its humanity, of its inner freedom, of its longing for peace, of its dignity?

If this were possible, would it not be worthwhile to live and work again? Let us try to become a morsel of this Europe which, at the moment, had to disappear. But let us not do it in words but in deeds. To serve and not to rule; to help and not to force; to love and not to harm, will be our task. Thus I was thinking.

I understood my thoughts. They had emerged after weeks of trial and need and now stood before me and helped me to clarify my problem of existence. On this Christmas Eve neither Camphill nor the movement existed. The future was shrouded but a will started to find its way.

Threefoldness is the hallmark of every living organism. Throughout the history of Camphill, forces of growth, development and metamorphosis have been experienced that have their foundation in the recognition of a threefold social structure corresponding to man as a being of body, soul and spirit. On the occasion of Camphill's twenty-first anniversary, Dr König described three great personalities that stood as "godfathers" to his inspirations: Amos Comenius, Count Zinsendorf, Robert Owen.

The following essay, written in 1965, expresses his fiery convictions drawn from 25 years of community life in the service of those in need of special care; convictions that inspired others.

The Three Essentials of Camphill

Looking back to the early beginnings twenty-five years ago, we can observe a slow uphill advance. It is by no means a story of success and splendour. It is a tale of trial and error, of hard labour and of many failures.

Twenty-five years is a long time! Much greater things have happened in the course of quarter of a century. But Camphill had to grow against many odds and — to begin with — under rather unfavourable conditions. It has, nevertheless, made its way and will continue to pursue its aims. The goal is still far ahead.

Materially we began with next to nothing. Around us was a foreign country and almost the whole world at war. We — a small band of refugees — were classified as "enemy aliens" and most of us had to spend many months in an internment camp. After our release the war gathered strength and fury and the country was fully occupied combating a deadly onslaught.

During this turmoil of "sweat and labour, of blood and human suffering" the seed of Camphill slowly began to sprout. The silent message of the handicapped child reached a number of parents, doctors, and teachers. Education authorities heard of our effort and sent some of their charges to Camphill. An increasing number of inquiries reached our office and the available space was soon unable to satisfy the demand.

We, therefore, tried to acquire or rent some neighbouring estates in order to enlarge our work. A few helpers and friends joined the original nucleus of people, but not nearly enough to carry the spreading task satisfactorily. There were far too many children for the handful of co-workers. Only by sheer grace, and the greatest sacrifice on the part of everyone, could this difficult period be surmounted. But gradually relief and help came.

The war changed into peace; frontiers were opened and young people came from the Continent to help us. More and more parents, relieved from the heavy burden of the war, supported our efforts, and some influential people gave us advice and counsel. The seed of Camphill had already grown into a small plant. Branches developed and attempted to sprout through their own strength.

And one day, a few buds began to appear on one or other twig of this tiny bush. They unfolded into flowers and radiated their beauty and scent into our hearts. These flowers were the inner victories of our external labour and work: the improvement we observed in some of the children, the peace slowly achieved in daily life, the silent wonder during the services on Sunday morning, the sudden understanding of the innermost nature of one or another of the children — these were the things that made our work worthwhile.

We gradually became aware of the beauty of these flowers. We began to realize that their radiance gave us strength and perseverance. But there were long stretches of time when the bush of Camphill had no flowers. The leaves of everyday life just continued to grow, but no further fresh buds appeared. Then suddenly and unexpectedly, a whole branch burst out again into blossom; and it even occurred a few times that all over the movement a sea of flowers unfolded in wondrous beauty. These were the times when the ideals of Camphill were strong enough to permeate our life and work. For these flowers are the essentials of Camphill which appear, shine forth and wither away again.

Some of the flowers, however, are fertilized and change into fruits . When this occurs, we can clearly observe the results of our labour. With each fruit we make another step in the understanding of our children, of our work and our task. These fruits will never perish. They remain, endure and feed our further efforts.

The essentials of Camphill are these fruits and flowers; when they fail to unfold and grow, Camphill will not be able to develop and to keep its pledge to the handicapped child.

Today the whole civilized world is aware that even severe mental handicap can be improved under remedial education. In schools, homes and hospitals remedial education, occupational therapy and therapeutic communities are already a general rule.

The handicapped child is no longer looked upon as an imbecile person and a burden to the community. Its human abilities are recognized and great efforts are being made to treat and train, to teach and help these children.

To us, as pupils of Rudolf Steiner, the child — whatever his mental condition may be — is more than his physical appearance may indicate. He is more than his body, more than his emotions, more than his spoken or unspoken words. He is even more than his achievements. In his appearance he is merely the outer shell of an infinite and eternal spiritual being.

What does this mean? We are convinced that every human being has his individual existence not only here on earth between birth and death, but that every child was a spiritual entity before he was born, and that every man will continue to live after he has passed through the gate of death. Thus, any kind of physical or mental handicap is not acquired by chance or misfortune. It has a definite meaning for the individual and is meant to change his life.

Like any other human being who has to battle with various diseases, the handicapped child also has to learn how to live with his ailment or to conquer it. As parents and teachers, our task is to appeal to the eternal being of the child, to make him recognize his destiny. However hidden his individuality may be and however covered up by the many layers of inability, lameness and uncontrolled emotions — we must try to break through these sheaths and reach the holy of holies in every man: the seat of his spiritual entity.

The conviction that every man carries this "I" in him and that this "I" is eternal, imperishable and of a spiritual nature, is fundamental for our approach to the child. He is our brother and our sister. He is equal to every other human being and equal to us. We do not deal with the *handicapped* child; we deal with the *child* who is handicapped.

Many of them are retarded, paralysed, epileptic, incompetent, lazy, abnormal or backward.

All this may be as it appears. The nucleus of the being, the inmost kernel of his existence is not only infinite; it is divine! It is part of the divinity to which it will return and from whence it came and will come again. His crippled and distorted life is but one among many such lives on his way back to the Father. We are all prodigal sons seeking our ways back to the house of the eternal ground of the world, the fountainhead of our existence. This is the first essential of Camphill.

And the second? Three times the Gospels relate the story of the young man who suffered from epilepsy sickness and whom the disciples could not heal. Only Christ — after having gone through the stage of Transfiguration — is able to cast out the evil spirit. And when the disciples asked him why they themselves were helpless, he replied: "Because of your little faith. For truly, I say to you, if you have faith as a grain of mustard seed, you will say to this mountain, 'Move from here to there,' and it will move; and nothing will be impossible to you." (Matt.17:20).

This saying should not be taken literally but spiritually. It simply indicates that man is endowed with a power which has creative possibilities. This power can build houses and temples; it paints pictures and forms sculptures; it is the same power which invented the wheel, spanned the first bridges over a river and trained horses. This is the power which can move mountains and has done so throughout mankind's evolution.

This inner force is not man's intellect nor his intelligence. It is his ability to transform nature. It is the creative force which changes wild sceneries into lovely landscapes; the force which tills the soil and invented the potter's wheel and the weaver's loom.

This creative power is gradually fading away. Our technical civilization no longer has any place for it. The gadgets and machines do all the "creative work" which every human being was called upon to do until the beginning of this century. This transformation is quite justified in the sphere of industrial production and everyday life. It is right to substitute central heating for an open fireplace and a washing machine for a wooden tub. It is already questionable whether a horse-drawn plough can be replaced by a tractor. And where a human being is concerned there should be no question whether machines can replace the creative ability of man. No teaching machine can be substituted for the teacher; no mechanical means for the direct contact between man and man.

The "grain of mustard seed" of creativity is one of the fundamentals in remedial education. It has to be renewed day after day in those who work with the handicapped child. This faith "to be able to move mountains" is the prerogative of the teacher and helper in the field of mental deficiency. He must acquire it, otherwise his work becomes stale.

Rudolf Steiner has drawn attention to this need in his lectures on curative education. He said: "Whatever you do when treating and educating a handicapped child — you will always interfere with his destiny. It is a real interference in the child's karma." We, as teachers and doctors, can only do the work for the retarded child if we engender in our souls the creative power which may be able to remove or at least lower the mountain of handicap.

To kindle this inner power should be the daily exercise of the teacher. He has to educate himself and to gain a steady certainty in his responsibility and conscientiousness: *His responsibility for the destiny of the handicapped child; his conscientiousness for the work with his child* — these are the two indispensable virtues of the curative teacher.

If the teacher and helper can achieve this, then spiritual sources are opened up and intuition will guide and replenish his labour. Every morning and evening the teacher must turn to this fountainhead of his existence; be it in prayer and meditation, or concentration and other mental exercises. Such inner education has to be pursued. Otherwise the teacher's strength will fail and his most precious gift, spiritual courage, will vanish.

As curative teachers we need undaunted energy and courage. Nothing but prayer and meditation can create this special faculty in the human soul of today. And when the disciples asked further why they were unable to cast out the evil spirit from the boy, Christ answered: "This kind cannot be drive forth by anything but prayer and fasting" (Mark 9:29).

Again — such words of Christ cannot be taken literally. We neither cast out spirits nor do we need to fast. "To cast out spirits" means to create a surrounding congenial to a handicapped child. It is an environment of loving peace and peaceful love. It is a house without noise and hurry, without restlessness and quarrel. And "to fast" means to forgo the various temptations today's life offers us: television, radio, drink, chatter, gossip and the many things that make life so difficult and unbearable. This type of everyday existence is the greatest enemy of the handicapped child.

If we are able to renounce these temptations and lead a life without that glamour, we do justice to the handicapped child by "praying and fasting".

Who will understand this? Today millions of cripples, disabled and impaired people are "entertained" all over the world by the evil powers of wireless and television. With the best of intentions the worst influence is thus brought to bear. None of our houses in Camphill has television; and the radio is only turned on when special occasions make it necessary.

The inner education of the teacher is the second essential of Camphill. His endurance and sacrifice, his continued care of the child and his attempt "to fast and pray", thereby creating "the grain of mustard seed" in his soul, is this second essential. We try to prepare it during our training courses. Not only knowledge is given to our students. They learn to kindle their creative forces and to make them into a continuous source of strength and sacrifice.

The third essential is the following: During the last two decades a new science has markedly moved into the foreground of common knowledge: sociology. Though it is an old science it had never been in the consciousness of the general public. But today everybody speaks about "human relations", "interpersonal relationships", "social psychology" etc. All this is due to the growing awareness that every human being is largely dependent on his environment and under the deep and direct influence of his fellow men.

We have learned to understand the lasting influence which a mother has on her baby. We know that no infant will grow up unharmed without the loving care and personal dependence he receives from his environment. We began to recognize the powerful character formation which a family extends over its members, and we have studied the influence of the larger community on each one of its members.

In fact, we have become convinced through an overwhelming number of observations that man is — to use a word from Aristotle — a *zoön politikon*, a social animal. (*Zoön* for the Greek was more "a living being" and not "an animal" in today's sense and meaning.) Man is a social being! We might almost say: Man can only be man when he is part of other human beings. An isolated man is unable to develop his humanity. Everyone is dependent on the other; he must communicate with the other and be recognized by the other. Every "I" needs his "you", every "me" needs his "him" or "her". This is true for every human being, for the sane as much as for the insane, for the clever as for the backward. The community, whichever form it takes, is the essential womb of man.

This social womb has several layers. The innermost one is the family, the second is represented by the village or the street and district of the town. The third layer is the community of the people who speak the same language. And the outermost and largest layer is the whole of mankind. Just as no embryo can live outside the womb and its layers so no born man can live outside the womb of human community. We are born out of one womb into the other;

from out of our mother's womb into the womb of society. And every infant has to adjust himself from the one environment to the other. If there is not enough loving guidance and gentle care, this adjustment will be difficult and sometimes even impossible.

Many handicapped children suffer severely under this maladjustment. The disappointment of the parents, the misunderstanding of the surrounding, the inability to interpret their strange appearance and odd behaviour drives them into isolation. This happens far more often than we realize. It is, therefore, one of the most essential conditions for remedial education and training to provide an adequate social womb with the appropriate layers of community living for handicapped children and adults. It is the basis for work with mentally afflicted people.

Since the beginning of Camphill, we were conscious of this basic need in our work. And we have never ceased to readjust our social structure and remodel it according to changing conditions.

Superficial observers and fleeting visitors often judge our way of life with a preconceived opinion. The fact that none of our co-workers receives a wage or salary is not an economic arrangement but part of our social endeavour to create the right environment for the handicapped person. We are convinced that we could not do our work in the same manner if we were employees and received a salary, because we know that work which is paid has lost its social value. No professional person can be paid for his services. As soon as it is paid, it is no longer a service! Wages (not money!) create a barrier between the one who receives and the one who pays. To give and to take is a matter of mutual human relationship; the true relationship goes as soon as wages intervene. Paid service is no service; paid love is no love; paid help has nothing to do with help.

If we begin to understand the tender connection which exists between services and social environment, a new light is shed on community for the education and care of handicapped people. This work will only succeed socially if salaries are not involved. Payments should be made in another form. They can be given as freely as the services which are rendered.

In the sphere of economy a true brotherhood must be established: a brotherhood of inequality and individual standards. Not everyone can live under similar conditions as his brother and sister. The earthly needs of men are different; yet men should learn to live in fraternity in spite of their different economic requirements.

There is, however, another social sphere where equality is necessary. This is the realm of the individual rights of people. The right to speak, to know and to do. A community of men can only function if these rights are properly observed. The realm of work — be it a school, a business, a factory or a hospital — will only be permeated by the good will of everybody if each member of this community *knows* the work of others or is free to inform himself about this work. He must also have the right to *say* how he thinks the work should be distributed, arranged and furthered. Everybody's voice must be heard. And, lastly, each co-worker must be given the opportunity to *do* the kind of work for which he thinks he is destined. Yet he cannot claim this right for himself without allowing the same privilege to all the others.

In the realm of human co-operation and togetherness equality of rights, not brotherhood, is indicated. The standard of living is an individual matter; it depends on personal needs and necessities. But the difference in creative faculties, talents and working capacities call for a sphere of common rights where equal justice is done to all.

A third realm remains in the social order; it is the sphere of privacy. Neither equality nor brotherhood should permeate this social realm. It is the place where man has to be anti-social and self-contained. It is not possible in our time to be continually social. If we would do so, we would soon lose our identity and individual existence. Some sphere of privacy must be provided for each single person in a working community. Whether he wants a private room or a space for his family is his own decision. One will prefer his own workbench, the other a small library for himself, a third some time for private studies. Liberty has to rule in this social realm — but not liberty alone. The single person must also let his conscience speak so that his demands remain in harmony with the needs of the community.

If step by step these spheres of social order are achieved and adapted to the conditions of life, order and harmony will permeate the community.

Fraternity lives in the sphere of economy.
Equality is needed in the realm of co-operation.
Liberty, supported by the voice of conscience, rules the element of privacy.

In such a community the handicapped child will feel accepted and secure; the backward and crippled adult will experience his humanity and each co-worker can find his place to live and work creatively. This kind of social order is the third essential of Camphill.

These are the three essentials which give the basis to our life and form the background to our work. They indicate the difference between Camphill and similar schools and homes for handicapped children.

These essentials are threefold in structure and it would be difficult to establish one or even two without attempting all three together. The three essentials are interwoven with one another. Regard for the spiritual nature of one's fellow man, the endeavour of one's inner development and the establishment of a true community are a trinity; they are a threefold unity.

This threefold ideal will hardly ever find fulfilment here on earth. It should be an aim we try to achieve and a goal for which we strive; but it lies in the nature of every ideal that it can never be fully attained. This is human destiny. Nevertheless, to attempt to find the way and to walk towards an ideal are necessary.

When this is done the right atmosphere is created, which is a fundamental need for every handicapped person, child or adult. It is an atmosphere of human striving and endeavour for spiritual ideals. The handicapped personality needs an environment which is permeated by higher values, spiritual and religious.

The child in need of special care asks for the renewal of his soul. But regeneration can only occur if the child's surrounding is filled with higher values like the three essentials of Camphill. A community longing for communion with the Spirit provides the true living breath for crippled, ill and handicapped people.

The renewal of the soul by the living breath of the Spirit is the ultimate aim of remedial education. It strives for the repeated presence of the Comforter, the Holy Spirit, who is the Healing Spirit. The three essentials are one of the means to create a social condition for the Healing Spirit to work. He has the power to make every child and every man "whole" again. But "whole" is not "healthy". The Holy Spirit restores the strength to take up one's cross and to walk along the path of individual destiny.

In a community striving for the three essentials the words of John the Baptist can be heard: "The crooked shall be made straight, and the rough ways shall be made smooth; and all flesh shall see the salvation of God."

Since that time, roughly thirty years ago, the provision for handicapped people has grown, improved, and in some cases, become similar to what Camphill attempts to offer today.

The wave of compassion that has swept the world since the mid-fifties has gone hand in hand with the realization that not only some are handicapped, but that today, more than ever, each human being is in need of "the Spirit that maketh whole".

The experience of loss of this spiritual homeland is accompanied by man's increasing dependence on the powers of technology that are advancing at a frightening pace, confronting him with an overwhelming realization of his responsibility for the planet earth today. The centres of Camphill also take part in the suffering of mankind as a whole. To be alert to the needs of the present time and to express this in deeds will require an unceasing effort from those who intend to carry the torch lit by Karl König.

Chapter 2

The history and development of Camphill

Friedwart Bock

Camphill began in 1939/40 when a small band of young refugees from Austria together with their mentor, Dr Karl König, found a house in the north-east of Scotland. Their new home was Camphill, a twenty-five acre estate seven miles from Aberdeen.

Karl König was a well known medical practitioner who had resolved to devote his energies to the needs of the handicapped child. While practising in Vienna a group of intellectuals and artists met in his study group — they studied Rudolf Steiner's Anthroposophy — and set their sights on establishing a community for handicapped people. The political oppression in Austria and Germany in 1938 made them apply in turn to France, Cyprus, Ireland and Britain. Just before the outbreak of the Second World War Britain opened its doors to them. Dr König arrived in London late in 1939 and wrote to his young friends on December 19:

Yesterday I returned from Scotland where Mr and Mrs Houghton had invited me to tell them of our plans. In their estate near Insch, Aberdeenshire, there is a vacant manse which they would like to acquire for our use. It would be suitable, to begin with, to accommodate us and fifteen to twenty children. During the first months we will be supplied with food. Dear friends, this Christmas we will permeate our hearts with good will for our work which shall become the working of the World Word.

We are permitted to look back with gratitude upon a destiny which has guided us with so much blessing. We look forward with joy to the work we want to accomplish. One by one the group from Europe arrived at Kirkton House. Though without electricity

Below left: Kirkton House near Insch, Aberdeenshire. Below right: Camphill House from the west.

Early days of Camphill.
1 Robin Linney; 2 -; 3 -;
4 -; 5 Christoph König; 6
Renate König; 7 Peter
Bergel; 8 Andreas König; 9
Veronica König.

1 Anke Weihs; 2 Peter
Roth; 3 Marie Korach; 4
Alix Roth; 5 -; 6 -; 7 Trude
Amann; 8 Willi Amann; 9
Alex Baum; 10 Thomas
Weihs; 11 -; 12 Renate
König; 13 Peter Bergel; 14
Robin Linney; 15 Karl
König; 16 Veronica König;
17 Andreas König; 18
Christoph König.

37

and heating they had made a home there. Children with special needs were taken in, and on May 28, 1939, the opening ceremony was performed in the small rectory overlooking the granite hills north of the River Don. The war began and following Dunkirk the group was classified as enemy aliens and the men interned.

1 Willi Amann; 2 Peter Roth; 3 Anke Weihs; 4 Thomas Weihs; 5 Alex Baum; 6 Tilla König; 7 Trude Amann; 8 Marie Korach; 9 Alix Roth.

1 Anke Weihs; 2 Peter Roth; 3 Marie Korach; 4 Alix Roth; 5 -; 6 -; 7 Trude Amann; 8 Willi Amann; 9 Tilla König; 10 Robert Linney; 11 Thomas Weihs; 12 Alex Baum; Christoph König; 14 -; 15 Renate König; 16 Peter Bergel; 17 Andreas König; 18 Veronica König.

38

A larger house was found, Camphill House on the Royal Deeside, and purchased by the publisher Mr W.F. Macmillan. It was let to Camphill at a nominal rental and all loans were repaid in 1943. In the absence of the men, the move was accomplished by the women, chiefly Tilla König, Alix Roth and Anke Weihs, and on June 1, 1940, the life and work of Camphill began. Later in the year the men returned from internment on the Isle of Man to find Camphill well established, and about twelve children in residence. In an interview with the *Aberdeen Press and Journal* on October 21, 1940, Dr König said:

> I have several English and refugee children here at present, but I hope to do something for Scottish children especially. I was told by the Board of Control in Edinburgh that this is the first private institution for such children in this country. In addition to twenty-four children we will be able to care for adults at a lodge and cottage on the estate. The children become part of a community under our system — and it is of course, a Christian community.

Profiles of some members of the founding group

Tilla König came from Silesia, Germany, and had a Moravian Brethren upbringing. Her work with children led her to Arlesheim, Switzerland, where she met Karl König. Both studied with Ita Wegman. After Tilla's marriage in 1929 they built up a curative educational home in Pilgramshain, Silesia, before moving to Vienna, and from there to Kirkton House, Aberdeenshire as refugees. They established Camphill in 1940. Her attitude to each person and each thing was an example for all who worked with her.

Alix Roth came from Vienna where she worked as a photographer. She met Anthroposophy in the youth group at Dr König's house, together with her brother and his friends. In Camphill she was at the centre of the nurses' work and vital in founding the work in Central Europe.

Anke Weihs went to Vienna in 1930 as a dancer. After meeting the youth group gathered around Dr König, she joined those who went to Scotland as refugees. Her contribution was outstanding by virtue of its creativity.

Trude Amann came from Vienna where she met the founding group before training in curative education at Arlesheim, Switzerland. What she learned there remained a source of inspiration for the therapeutic work to come.

Barbara Lipsker, a member of the Vienna youth group, joined the work in Camphill shortly after it began. She has been for many years the principal at Glencraig, Northern Ireland.

Marie Korach came in contact with Alix and Peter Roth at an early age. As a member of Dr König's youth group she joined the early founders in Kirkton House and has made a manifold contribution to the work.

Thomas Weihs studied medicine in Vienna where he met the youth group together with his friend Peter Roth. After graduating in Basel he came to Britain on the last boat before the war and joined the little community in Kirkton House. He worked in agriculture and eventually took over the medical curative work from Dr König.

Carlo Pietzner came from Vienna. He became a member of the youth group while training as an artist and joined the small community after its move to Camphill House in 1941. He was

Clockwise from top left: Tilla König, née Maasberg (born March 9, 1902 at Gnadenfrei, Silesia, died July 17 1983 at Camphill Alpha, South Africa). Alix Roth (born June 24, 1916 at Vienna, died May 25, 1987 at Aigues Vertes, Geneva). Trude Amann, née Blau (born March 23, 1915 at Vienna, died March 28, 1987 Camphill, Aberdeen). Anke Weihs, née Nederhoed (born June 30, 1914 at Melbourne, Australia, died August 27, 1987 at Camphill, Aberdeen).

40

central in the founding of the work in Glencraig, Northern Ireland, and from 1960, in the United States.

Alex Baum was one of the first to join the youth group around Dr König in 1936. He studied chemistry but had to flee to Britain to escape Nazi oppression and linked up with the other founders at Kirkton House in 1939. The teaching impulse and the furthering of eurythmy were his particular concerns.

Peter Roth began his medical studies at eighteen and found his way to Dr König's youth group. Later he became a priest of The Christian Community and pioneered the Camphill village work at Botton (England), where he is an influence to this day.

Hans and Lisl Schauder, and *Willi Amann* were also members of the founding group, first in Vienna and then in the north-east of Scotland. They left in 1943 to start Garvald in Peeblesshire, south of Edinburgh.

From left: Thomas Weihs (born April 30, 1914 at Vienna, died June 19, 1983 at Camphill, Aberdeen). Carlo Pietzner (born January 26, 1915 at Vienna, died April 17, 1986 at Copake, New York). Alex Baum (born August 31, 1910 at Vienna, died November 4, 1975 at Munich).

So the first decade began. The preliminary development at Kirkton House was now set to grow and develop at Camphill. At a time when the War escalated in Europe, North Africa and Asia, the plight of the children in need of special care was brought to Karl König and his friends. The small community at Camphill thrived. In 1942 Heathcot House on the south side of the river was rented to cope with the constant need for further places. In these early years most of the children were sent privately to Camphill.

In April 1944, Murtle House was acquired with its thirty-five acres. With three separate properties there would be no pressure of numbers; but then a group of lads who had been before the juvenile courts and presented various degrees of delinquency, came to Camphill.

Top: Heathcote House, Aberdeenshire. Above: Birthday celebration at Heathcote House with Tilla König. Murtle House, Aberdeenshire, from the south (above right) and from the north (right).

They benefited directly from the presence of the more frail and handicapped children, but Camphill did not have the facilities to give them what they needed. In March 1945, Newton Dee, an estate of 170 acres, came on the market, and was acquired with the help of Helen Macmillan, who was later repaid. The farm and workshops at Newton Dee provided ideal facilities for the lads.

In 1947–48, St John's School, a small Waldorf school for co-workers' children, and normal children from Aberdeen, opened at Murtle. Three years later all pupils and staff children were included in this schooling because Karl König recognized the potential benefit of Waldorf teaching for all children.

Just before the end of the foundation decade, Camphill featured in an article in an illustrated weekly, the *Picture Post*. In the April 30, 1949 issue, Fyfe Robertson wrote:

Individual treatment is the chief secret of Camphill's successes. The basic treatment for all is good, naturally-grown, balanced food; intelligent medical care; a serene and

St John's play at Murtle, 1952, with view of the Dee valley.

Newton Dee farmhouse from the south-west (top) and Newton Dee House from the south-east (right).

44

regular life, and above all, the affection which these children need and which can sometimes make them flower wonderfully.

Of the 180 children at these schools, about a hundred are unable to use speech properly, and hardly any of the children can move harmoniously and gracefully. Both conditions are concerned with voluntary muscle control, and Camphill uses the Steiner method to deal with this. Music, colour, and "curative eurythmy" — in which the children are taught, by special alphabet movements of the limbs, to "speak" with the whole body — are bringing results. If one can loosen the speech organs, the main battle is won — and the locked personality will be partly freed. It really should not surprise us that speech, which has been so powerful in emancipating and bemusing the mind of man, acts in this way as an integrator of the personality.

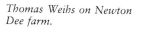

Thomas Weihs on Newton Dee farm.

Picture map of Camphill, Murtle, Newton Dee, Cairnlee and Heathcote. Cairnlee House from the west (below left). Murtle House, after the play, St John's Day, 1952 (below right).

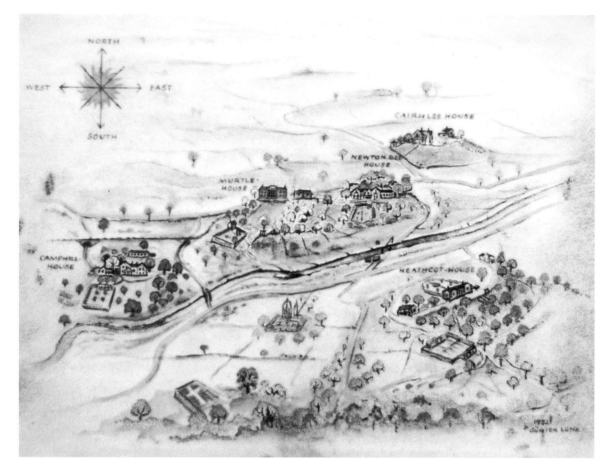

The Sheiling, Ringwood, England (top). Dawn Farm, Hermanus, South Africa (bottom left). Thornbury House, Bristol, England (bottom right).

Opposite, top: The Lehenhof, Lake Constance, Germany.

Opposite bottom: Downingtown, Pennsylvania, United States.

The *Picture Post* article included many photographs and brought a spate of inquiries. A waiting list for children had to be set up.

In October 1949, a Camphill Seminar Course began for young people who wanted to learn about curative education. Many hundreds have completed the Camphill Seminar in the twelve centres where the course is now conducted. The seminar has a seminal quality and has been vital to the growth of the movement.

The second decade, from 1950 to 1959, began with the acquisition of the fifth estate, Cairnlee, initially for the use of severely disturbed adolescent girls. Age groups were segregated into different houses and estates right up to 1964, after which a wide spectrum of ages was placed in every house.

There were now 240 children, with a roughly equal number of private and local authority referrals, but local authority referrals were to outstrip the private ones quite soon. Karl König strongly maintained the educability of every child, however handicapped. Legislation caught up with this view only very gradually, beginning in 1959, and established the principle of education for *all* children in 1974.

The main feature of Camphill's second decade was the move into England, Ireland, South Africa, Germany and the United States. Mrs Redman of South Africa had seen the *Picture Post* article and asked Dr König to help in her country. In 1951 a Camphill-trained teacher went out to Dawn Farm, Hermanus. Calls from individual parents or parents' associations were met by Camphill opening centres in England at the Sheiling, Ringwood and Thornbury, Bristol, in 1951, and at Glencraig in Northern Ireland in 1953. The step to continental Europe was made when work with spastic children was established at Brachenreuthe, Germany, in 1958, following a similar call. In 1959 Camphill was asked to take over an existing small curative home in

Below: Thornbury Park, Bristol, England.

Top: Brachenreuthe, Germany, looking towards Lake Constance.
Below: The opening of Föhrenbühl, Lake Constance, Germany, 1963.

Downingtown, Pennsylvania, from an elderly couple, and this led to the rapid growth of the work in the United States during the 1960s. During the same year Christophorus, Holland, a small home school established six years earlier, joined the Camphill family. During this phase the Camphill Movement, a network of identity embracing all the Camphill centres, was born.

A significant diversification of the Camphill work took place in 1954 with the establishment of the first village for handicapped adults, in Botton on the Yorkshire moors. Again it was parents who prompted this development by their insistence that Camphill could do this. The base for village work had been created at Newton Dee as early as 1945. In 1952 Karl König wrote in a report:

> I would wish that in later years Camphill might become a place where the conscience for curative education will be kept awake — a place where the true destiny of the handicapped child will always be known . . . It should always grow into a place where those children, not attaining sufficient improvements to go out into the world, could remain and have a sheltered yet useful life. They could do some limited work in the various kitchens and workshops, the houses, the farm, and the gardens. They should

Top left: Whitsun pageant
at Camphill Hall, Scotland.
Top right: Barbara
Lipsker, Anke Weihs, Peter
Roth, Kate Roth, Thomas
Weihs, at Camphill
Scotland, September 1962.

Left and bottom left:
Botton Hall, Yorkshire.
Below: Glencraig,
Northern Ireland.

51

Right: Donald Perkins (with beret) at Camphill

Below: Hall with Murtle House, from the south. Below right: St John's festival. Bottom: King Arthur pageant, Whitsun 1979.

not live in dormitories but in small houses in the lap of the family to which they belong and where they feel safe and secure. Thus around each one of our houses a very small village should grow with four or five small houses occupied by a few families finding their place in life and work. The idea of a true village community, growing ever deeper, will have to find roots in our efforts.

The opening of Camphill Hall, September 22, 1962. Left: Karl König and Alix Roth. Below: Gabor Tallo, James Downie-Campbell and Thomas Weihs.

Bottom: Carlo Pietzner.

His vision became reality two years later. It is a remarkable stroke of destiny that the Botton property which was selected for the first village was the Macmillan family's former country estate.

The destiny of a movement is bound up with that of its founder. Camphill's second decade saw Dr König's serious illness in 1955 and his decision in 1957 to pass on his duties as superintendent of the Camphill Rudolf Steiner Schools to Thomas Weihs, while he remained as consultant. Dr König also took up the task of chairman of the Camphill Movement. As an organ of the Camphill Movement the *Cresset* was launched, a quarterly journal that appeared for eighteen years. One part of the *Cresset's* title reads:

> The *Cresset* shall be an expression of the Camphill movement's innermost urge to help carry forward the glow brought to life by Rudolf Steiner to the end that the contemporary knowledge of man be enflamed by the fire of love.

The third decade (1960–69) began with Newton Dee's change of task; moving from a school setting for adolescent handicapped boys to become the second major village for adults. The following year, in 1961, a village was established near Geneva, Switzerland.

Hans Heinrich Engel was active as a physician in Scotland and Northern Ireland for many years before his untimely death in 1973.

The nodal point in this middle decade was the laying of the foundation stone of the Camphill Hall on July 1, 1961. This year also marked the centenary of Rudolf Steiner's birth and the twenty-first anniversary of the founding of Camphill. The building of the hall became the expression of the concerted efforts of the movement to build a space where conferences could be held; where the work could be developed and deepened. The opening of the Camphill Hall in September 1962, was at the same time a tribute by the movement to its founder whose sixtieth birthday fell in that month.

Two years later, in 1964, Dr König relinquished his place as chairman of the Camphill Movement, a truly exemplary move, having divided the Movement into six regions, each with its own chairman. He moved back to Germany to strengthen the work there and to chair a region comprising the centres around Lake Constance and Lake Geneva. Thus the Camphill Movement was regionalized and the administration decentralized. Camphill Aberdeen was no longer the centre of the movement, yet it has long remained a focal point.

The work in Germany made great strides during 1964 when Föhrenbühl opened its doors for many children as a neighbour to Brachenreuthe. The following year, in September, the first German village, at the Lehenhof, was opened by Dr König.

When Karl König died in March 1966, he had seen his vision of a community *with* the handicapped person come to reality. He had seen the expansion of the movement from its central position, and then to the development of a decentralized but inter-relating autonomy, which is a true deed of brotherliness. This development of the movement and the death of its founder stand as the mid points of its fifty-year history.

In 1966 a village was founded at Vidaråsen, Norway, following a first unsuccessful attempt twelve years earlier. Now Camphill had a Scandinavian region, which has seen a string of villages develop in subsequent years.

The fourth ten-year period, the seventies, began with the Sylvia-Koti School in Finland joining the Camphill movement in 1970, making it the easternmost centre, and the one closest to

54

Russia. Through the personal initiative of a couple from the Ringwood centre, a small Camphill school for black children was established in Botswana in 1974: Camphill Rankoromane.

The 1970s saw growth in the work with adolescents and young adults: Coleg Elidyr in Wales, Templehill, Blair Drummond, Corbenic and Beannachar in Scotland, together with a school at Ochil Tower. In 1976 a village was established at Liebensfels, Austria, thirty-eight years after Karl König and his young friends had to leave their homeland to found and establish the work in Scotland.

Thomas Weihs's book *Children in Need of Special Care* was published in 1971, and remains a much sought after book for parents, students, teachers and specialists. It expresses Camphill's therapeutic principles and has gone through editions in Britain and America, as well as being translated into Spanish, Portuguese, Italian, German, French and Japanese. In 1975 *Camphill Correspondence* was first published as the second Camphill journal.

The Camphill Eurythmy School began at Ringwood in 1970, and later also in Botton. The eurythmy training is fully integrated into the life of both centres, and many talented young people are trained for artistic and therapeutic work within and outside Camphill.

In 1979 Camphill became a full member of the Konferenz for Curative Education and Social Therapy at Dornach, Switzerland. This body embraces all the work done in this field in the name of Rudolf Steiner.

A Camphill village started in Le Béal, France in May 1979. The French authorities accepted the Camphill Seminar certificate as equivalent to the diploma in special education. Another Camphill village began in Angaia, Brazil, during the same year.

In the last decade further diversification took place, including work with the elderly and with care units in the villages. A growth of urban communities is also characteristic of the 1980s. In England local authorities invited Camphill to develop a centre within the town perimeter at Milton Keynes, and at Middlesborough.

A further village started at Sauk Centre, Minnesota, in 1980 and in Sweden, Staffansgården, a village which had existed for nine years, became a Camphill village in 1983. In Scotland, Loch Arthur village began near Dumfries in 1984. In 1988 the first community for young adults, Soltane, was acquired in America. This development signalled a new step for the region.

An increase in government regulations relating to the care of the handicapped took place during the decade. These addressed questions of staff qualifications, registration of centres and led to restrictions on co-workers from abroad working in Camphill centres. National associations were formed throughout the movement to act for the centres, and the advice and help of external council members and directors is increasingly required.

While Camphill has extended its work world-wide, the circle of supporters also grows. A first international meeting of Camphill board (council) members took place at Ringwood in 1987 with eighty delegates and a further meeting took place in the anniversary year at Camphill Aberdeen.

The 1980s were a period when several of the founder group of Camphill pioneers died, all well into their seventies. Thomas Weihs died in 1983, Carlo Pietzner in 1986, Trude Amann, Alix Roth and Anke Weihs in 1987. They leave a wide field of tasks to the coming generations.

Public honours were awarded to several friends for their, and Camphill's, contribution to the work with the handicapped. In Germany Karl König received the Tutzing Star on October 27, 1963, and Ursula Herberg the BVK; in Britain, Peter Roth received the OBE, and Barbara Lipsker, Ann Harris and Lotte Sahlmann MBEs.

The Camphill movement with its seventy-two centres is now grouped into seven regions: Scotland, England & Wales, Ireland, Scandinavia, Central Europe, North America, and Southern Africa.

Chapter 3

Community perspectives
Camphill and Anthroposophy

Henning Hansmann

The work of Camphill has grown out of the spirit of Anthroposophy and is rooted in the soil of human society and the living earth. Its environment is the "air", the light and darkness, and the many colours weaving in between, of human destiny. The despair and love, human failure and the ever-renewing strength of idealism, pain and joy, and the striving to create an inner equilibrium in the soul, are the storms and gentle breeze, the hail and the warm rain, the biting frost and the mellow thaw of spring in which the living tree of Camphill has its being. Its leaves and blossoms unfold towards the nourishing light and the healing spirit of the cosmos. The sap is provided by the very life blood of the many individuals who become part of the being of the Camphill community. The fruit it develops grows out of individual effort and striving that unites with the striving of the Camphill community and may receive the love and grace of the spirit. Such fruit is offered to be consumed as "nourishment" or to fall back to the ground to renew the earth's fertility. Such fruit then becomes destiny and fulfilment of human individuals.

Camphill is part of the anthroposophical movement inspired by Rudolf Steiner (1861–1925). Steiner conceived Anthroposophy as a new wisdom of the spiritual, mental and physical nature of man; a wisdom that does not remain as merely abstract knowledge but kindles motivation and creativity. His teaching took up the heritage of the great European thinkers and philosophers and was influenced by developments in the natural sciences. Rudolf Steiner was one of those exceptional individuals in human history who could encompass the knowledge of their time, and he united this knowledge with his deep spiritual experience out of which his own teaching was born. Anthroposophy, as he taught it, is imbued with Christian faith born out of a spiritual perception of the present day working of Christ in each human being, in human society, and in the life of the whole earth. It opens up a new understanding of science as well as social questions. It also provides inspiration for the knowledge and practice of healing in medical and educational work, in agriculture, and many other fields of human endeavour.*

Rudolf Steiner foresaw the developments of this century. As far back as 1906, he spoke to a small group of contemporaries of the danger that the earth could be destroyed by the thoughtlessness and lack of love of man. He saw an imminent need for a renewal of the living forces of the earth and thought that the necessary new life forces could be created, not by the individual alone but only by communities in which individuals would unite and selflessly devote themselves to the task of creating healing forces within social life and for the very soil of the earth. He said that mankind is dancing on the edge of the abyss, but is not aware of it. Now, at the end of the century, mankind is aware of it, but we are still dancing on the edge.

Camphill is one of the manifestations of the Christian spirit of Anthroposophy. Since its inception during the Second World War, a growing number of mostly young people have come to live and work in the Camphill centres throughout the world. Many come out of their heart's longing to do something for the good of mankind. Some know about Anthroposophy, others meet it in the centres, but for each one the work with children, young people or adults who suffer from handicaps or deprivation, or with frail and old people, leads to a powerful encounter

* Rudolf Steiner's collected works are published by Rudolf Steiner Verlag, Dornach, Switzerland, and comprise more than three hundred volumes; the first forty-five are his written works including many collected essays and letters; the second part contains more than four thousand lectures, and the third part consists of reproductions of his artistic work including his architecture and sculpture. The lectures are mainly printed from shorthand reports which he seldom had time to edit. Rudolf Steiner Press, London, and Anthroposophical Press, New York, publish his works in English.

with his own shortcomings and frailties. The pain of this encounter and the longing to find new ways of healing, creates a thirst and hunger to drink from the well-spring and eat of the food that Anthroposophy can offer. The well-spring can be found in the renewal of artistic creativity, which finds expression both in daily work and life, and in the festivals that mark the seasons of the year. As long as human beings have lived on earth such festivals have served to unite with the spirit and give meaning to birth and death and the renewal of life. The bread that Anthroposophy offers is a new way of thinking that in no way contradicts modern sciences, but extends them. Anthroposophical science is firmly based on clear and devoted observation of the natural and human world and is at all times aware of the observer, that is, the human being himself. The phenomena of the world become clearer to the degree to which the observer's own thinking has become selfless, consistent and loving. It requires an attitude of acceptance that we, each one, are part of the world and part of one another. It calls for a Christian will which accepts responsibility for our thoughts and deeds and even for our feelings and emotional life. Such an attitude can become a way of life for every individual no matter what profession is followed or status held.

The observation of nature in all its glory and of our human existence on earth then leads us to an awareness that it cannot explain our origin. Natural science cannot explain how it comes about that every child has a human form. All it can do is explain such things as why people have a different colour of hair or skin, or are large or small. The human form itself, which is also spoken of as the Image of Man being created according to the Image of God, remains a mystery to a science that limits itself to outer observation. Equally, it cannot explain what happens to the individual who was striving and experienced suffering and joy in life, after he has passed through the gate of death. Science can observe only how the body becomes a corpse, subject to physical and chemical reactions which quickly dissolve the human form. Out of such observations arises a longing in the heart of each human being which can be expressed in the questions: "Where does my inner being come from?" "Who has led me into this life and presents me every day with the situations of my destiny?" "Where do we go to after our death?" This longing of the human heart can no longer be stilled by the teachings of ancient traditions, however great, wonderful and true they may be. We have a need to learn to know for ourselves through our own observation and experience where we come from, where we go to, and how we relate to that world of the spirit which encompasses the world of man and nature.

At the beginning of the century it was generally taboo to speak of spiritual experience. Rudolf Steiner knew that this would change by the end of the century and therefore offered Anthroposophy, the wisdom of man, which is a new science and philosophy, and includes the observation of both natural and spiritual experience. He predicted that by the end of the century the longing for spiritual experience would have increased to the extent that one could read about it in every newspaper. He made us aware that for many individuals spiritual experiences would, as it were, break into their lives and could become to them a profound disturbance. Others would long to have extra-sensory experiences induced by different kinds of malpractice. He warned that all spiritual experience which is tinged by self-satisfaction or a wish for personal gain is destructive. It creates mental imbalance and consequently social suffering. Therefore, anthroposophical science approaches spiritual development and experience on the same basis that is required for a sound and healthy natural science. Thinking needs to become selfless so that spiritual experience can be understood with a healthy human mind and with common sense.

The guidance Anthroposophy offers leaves the individual free because clear thinking and the observation of the world and the inner self provide a basis of awareness. Individual human beings can then be aware of each step in their personal development. Therefore, we no longer need gurus or father figures to tell us what to do. What we need are "sisters and brothers," friends who will warmly and clearly reflect each other so that a healthy self knowledge is gained and at the same time encouragement found.

This new way of self development is supported and strengthened through the practice and enjoyment of art. To practice an art — even quite modestly without becoming an accomplished artist — means to work at the harmonizing of the emotional life. It helps overcome personal sympathies and antipathies and enables one to approach the world with greater understanding, love and empathy. Rudolf Steiner drew our attention to a painful equation, saying that to the same extent to which mankind lacks art, his social existence is filled with lies. The need of the human soul to be creative finds its healthy fulfilment in artistic expression. If this is denied in education and social life it will be perverted into the creation of lies. At present our world is pervaded by lies which are an expression of political and commercial power-drives which induce fear. Yet underneath that decaying outer layer is the longing of the individual heart to develop healthy imaginations and true expressions of the human soul born on the wings of beauty, and to foster healthy human development. Thus, modern art is no longer inspired from above, as it was in former times, but becomes a creative act of raising the human existence anew to the spirit from where we came and to which we return. This helps to build a future human society.

Anthroposophy adds to these new approaches to science and art a renewal of religious life. Faith need no longer be blind but can be based on knowing and understanding, even if this knowledge of the revelations of the divine remains limited. The personal experience of spiritual realities provides a basis of a new faith. In our time there are many examples of men and women who have gone through great hardship and deprivation and have come out of it strong and radiant with love. In each one the secret source of inner strength was the acceptance of personal destiny, suffering, and the determination to love the human being despite the fact that he can appear as jailer or torturer. It requires inner activity of faith which holds on to the divine in the other human being when that divine spark is at times buried and the other person seems to have alienated himself from his own spirit.

Working and sharing life with children and young or older people who suffer from handicaps, deprivation and sometimes abuse, helps to kindle this new faith. The acceptance of destiny creates a strength of will that can never be broken. It helps to be aware of Christ who lives in every human being and experiences his suffering and joy. It fills the human will with warmth and creates motivation to change what can be changed and brings healing into life situations. The new faith will permeate shared worship — and the celebration of the festivals belongs to this — as well as work and personal life.

Anthroposophy, which inspires Camphill, unites science, art and religion. It is the wellspring of our life and work as a community that unites us in freedom and human warmth. Compared with the whole of mankind, Camphill's contribution to the renewal of social life and the living forces of the earth is small indeed. Yet we have faith that our attempts — faltering though they may be — are part of the yeast that will make the dough of human society rise into a human loaf.

Three pillars

Barbara Lipsker

In an apocalyptic time like our present century, which has seen two world wars with an ultimate measure of suffering, which has brought forth staggering achievements in science, a time of danger and chaos, of blackest darkness and brightest flashes of light and promise — in such a time the toil of our existence is torn up, ploughed by the mighty world powers, open to receive new seeds for the future of our earth and of mankind. Perhaps one may look at the impulse of Camphill as one such seed.

Three major ingredients that gave and give life-power to that seed are:
—the willingness to develop a renewed quality of listening, free from one's own personal "opinion", from one's own personal directive will impulses, so that a greater truth, an "objective" answer, may be perceived;
—the certainty that any form of Camphill life would shape itself together with disadvantaged, handicapped or human beings with exceptional needs;
—the preparedness to live as a community and to share life in a brotherly way.

The overall aim is contained in these three ingredients: to strive to work in a way that will help towards bringing about the good on earth.

The first ingredient came to expression in the Bible Evening, about which Deborah Hudson has written later in this chapter.

The second ingredient has found particular expression in the "college meeting". This is a gathering of all those who are concerned with a particular child. Putting together all the known facts about the child, adding our own observations into the smallest details, our own involvement, shades of mutual relationship, all this will culminate in the question: what is truly "wrong" with the child? If we have been careful, and inwardly active enough, an image of the child will present itself in our midst in its full integrity and wholeness, against which we can recognize any aberration. In that compassionate experience the will to help and heal is born and insight is gained for the necessary therapy. Such a college meeting requires the greatest earnestness and reverence; it means to touch and influence the meaning of an individual destiny entrusted into our care. It is here where our own honest effort towards self-discipline and self-knowledge come into question — it is a search for truth. Again, this works into our daily life: to search for understanding of the wholeness which needs to be found behind the symptoms. This requires wakefulness, reverence to the smallest detail in observation, but also in our actual activity: devotion to the smallest thing, to the most (apparently!) insignificant action — this will kindle moral strength and responsibility. Also in our studies, in all our spiritual work when we want to gain knowledge and understanding of man and the world, this moral strength is needed, if it is to result in helping deeds and not remain intellectual knowledge alone; in all research work this moral strength is needed if results are to contribute to the good of the world and not its destruction. The form of the college meeting can be applied towards gaining understanding in *any* problem, or insight in *any* research or study. The presence of our handicapped companions is a constant challenge to the activity of our spiritual life, to our honest efforts for self-knowledge, to the warmth and enthusiasm of our moral impulses. They speak to our heart in which true understanding is to be born, not in our intellect alone.

The preparedness to live as a community and to share in a brotherly way has influenced life in Camphill in a very definite way. If it is in the social sphere that we are equal as *human* beings, if in the realm of spiritual life the free decision and choice of each individual human being for personal spiritual activity is essential, then there is a third realm, the practical realm of our work and our needs and there the *otherness* of each person is to be met and respected.

Human beings are different from one another. Accordingly, their needs, hopes and demands will be different. To learn to direct one's attention to the needs of one's fellow man, to be willing to put the result of one's work at the disposal of such needs instead of putting it into one's own pocket as regular wages, trusting that thereby one's own needs will be seen to as well, frees the power of brotherly love to one another, prevents hierarchical ambitions and "rights" and strengthens social responsibility. It is here where an answer may be looked for to the question: "Am I my brother's keeper?"

> The following words by Rudolf Steiner may be quoted in connection with the foregoing:
> The well-being of a community will be the greater the less the individual claims the proceeds of his own work and the more he makes them over to his fellow workers, and the more his own requirements are satisfied not out of his own work, but out of the work done by others.*
> The healthy social life is found when in the mirror of each human soul the whole community finds its reflection, and when in the community the virtue of each one is living.†

All foregoing descriptions are given in the full awareness that they refer to ideals which will take a long time to achieve fully. However, a beginning must be made in actual practising. Camphill has been guided by these ideals for some fifty years now, trusting that despite struggles, failures and repeated heart-searching, a contribution may be given to those greater powers in the world who work towards the realization of the good on earth.

Metamorphosis and being

Penelope Roberts

George came home from work a little early. It had been a very hot day and he'd been mowing lawns since two in the afternoon. George was good at mowing lawns. He didn't have to concentrate so hard on every movement of his big, stiff hands . . . like getting dressed in the morning. It was more work to get his fingers to button every button of his shirt correctly than to mow a whole lawn. Still, he wasn't as easy-going about it as he had been a few years ago, before the accident with the stone. Then he'd been in hospital for days with patches over both his eyes. Lots of people had come to visit, to read or play music to him. But they had been afraid about his eye and that made him afraid too. He'd been lucky, though, and the eye was all right. And he knew how much everyone cared. Since then his eye sometimes bothered him a bit and he worried about it. It was hard not being able to talk about it, and his attempts only produced grunts and bellows. Of course everyone tried to understand and help, but it must be different if you can speak. Well, that was a long time ago. Now he wore goggles when he mowed lawns.

George lurched into the house and started up the stairs to get cleaned up for dinner. He noticed that there was something at the top. Suddenly there was a crash and a scream. George stumbled up the steps, managing to catch the baby just as she was bumping down. Terrified, he picked her up around the tummy with his huge, powerful hands. He was so strong. He didn't know if he could hold her without hurting her, making her cry more. He concentrated on keeping his hands from squeezing too hard. The baby couldn't talk either. They both smiled.

George is a friend of mine. For years I carried this picture of him holding my daughter like a treasure in his great hands. It helped me through many other times when in his terrible speechless frustration he would become a raging bull, lashing out even at those he loved the most. And many times I asked myself: "Who is George, this friend of mine?"

How many times in the history of man have we asked: "What is a human being?" How

* The "Fundamental Social Law" from *Anthroposophy and the Social Question.*

† The "Motto of the Social Ethic" from Rudolf Steiner to Edith Maryon, November 1920.

do we define humanity? What is it that makes us recognize the humanity of another? Countless philosophers and scientists have made the attempt to understand, while generation after generation of ordinary men and women, struggling to find meaning in life, have asked the same questions.

For some reason that subtle entity we call "humanity" seems to shine the brightest when it struggles the most. Perhaps that is why Karl König was so deeply overcome when he saw the handicapped child in Switzerland making its uncertain way so intently around the spiral Advent Garden.

Camphill was born out of the agony of the Third Reich in Germany, the Nazi regime, an era of evil if ever there was one. Yet this evil, oddly enough, sprang from an ideal, the ideal of the superman, the perfect human being.

Just in these years, however, there were human beings who had a different understanding of the pure blood and the whole body. They saw clearly that Hitler in his fanatic idealism had taken the highest picture of humanity and applied it in a completely materialistic way to the concept of heredity. He assumed that the human ideal belonged to one pure race and was passed down through the generations. These others, students of Rudolf Steiner, also held to an ideal image of humanity. For them, however, this was not a visible, racial concept. Through the insight of Anthroposophy they had learned to understand that the human *archetype*, the perfect image of man, is a *spiritual* entity to which *every* human being is related, regardless of race or any other aspect of his or her bodily constitution.

This human archetype is connected with the cosmic archetype expressed in the heavens, the twelvefoldness of the zodiac and the sevenfoldness of the planets. It is related to the kingdoms of nature, stone, plant and animal. It is also an expression of the gestures and even the sacrifices of high spiritual beings who have been active since the dawn of creation. Above all, it is the image of God. God created man in his own image, which is also the image of creation, the Word. The pure body and the pure blood are those of Christ in every human being. Here on earth the perfection is never achieved. Only to a degree, some more this way, some more that, does any living person outwardly manifest the perfection of the spiritual archetype.

Karl König was one of those who seemed to experience the spiritual image of man behind every human being, especially those whose outward appearance or behaviour was the most disturbed. He always saw what was being hindered from coming to full expression. For this reason he was a great healer, but he saw further; he did not stop at being a doctor; he saw another step to be taken.

In the thirties in Germany Hitler's ideals engendered fear and hatred and eventually the dehumanization of social life. What would be the possibilities for social life if men and women were to try to build a society based on the spiritual image of man as described by Rudolf Steiner? Karl König and his friends embarked on a social experiment which is still in process.

For eighteen years I have been a co-worker in Camphill. I can try to tell why I came and why I stayed so long. It has to do with the image of man and the social experiment.

For a few years I managed to bathe in the warmth and comfort that poured so generously from my village friends at Copake. But as things happen, there came the moment for accounting. One day I had to face the fact that actually I could also do something in return. With real shame I realized that I had been free-loading, imbibing love as though it were my due and doing very little to deserve it. Thus began my slow, precarious path of inner change. I was on the way to becoming. I realized that the possibility to experience, through the community around me, the need to change, was an essential factor of Camphill.

I believe that a fundamental principle of Camphill has to do with the polarity between what I shall call "metamorphosis" on the one hand and "essential being" on the other — a tension between the ever-evolving state of man and his society on earth and the eternal, or archetypal realities which exist in the spirit. Hence the paradox that the villagers seemed to see my true being and yet it was they who in the end compelled me to try to improve certain characteristics of my temporal being, my everyday self. This is a positive dynamic in community life. The challenge is to discover those aspects of community life which enhance the eternal image and how the individual or the community recognizes its development, its need to change.

The single human being cannot be truly human and therefore cannot be whole and healthy if he does not relate to other human beings. Only through others do we experience ourselves objectively. Through them we can realize our greatest potential, but they can also bring out our worst failings. If we have the encouragement and the will to overcome the latter for the sake of the former, then we begin to clear away some of the obstacles in front of us. We become more fully ourselves. Karl König believed that if many human beings could fight for and stand for the best in one another, social life would change. Anything could be done.

What matters is not simply living together, but the way, the form, of living together. The human being has certain attributes in common with all other human beings. He has a body, a soul and a spirit. He also thinks, he feels and he acts or does. Depending on the *social* context he may develop one of these attributes more than the others. For instance, a community of migrant workers has very little opportunity to develop an intellectual, cultural life as all their strength goes to the picking of crops from dawn to dusk and the little money they earn is saved to be taken home. On the other hand, a community of political prisoners may be forced to create a strong social interaction in order to counteract the boredom of empty, workless hours. There are many accounts of the "universities" that were set up in the prison camps of the Second World War. A community with strong religious leanings provides the individual with opportunities to develop his devotional nature. A harsh environment like the slums of New York creates the gangs which are loyal to one another but basically at war with everything else. Of course these are all exaggerated examples and even within them every individual will develop differently. All the same it seems obvious that the more fully social life can provide the opportunities for individuals to express themselves in different ways, calling forth different parts of their being (head, heart, limbs for example), the more balanced and rounded will those individuals be. This is most striking with those who are not so mobile in society, such as our disabled or disturbed friends. The most moving experiences I have had in my years in Camphill have had to do with the surprises that come when a person who is difficult in one realm of life suddenly shines in another.

Through the possibilities of encounter in the many forms and settings, discoveries are made. "Is that also you? I had no idea!" Every new aspect of the community has the potential to light up the individual in his greater completeness and consequently to strengthen bonds from one to the other. Because the forms of the community are derived from the human form (again: head, heart and limbs) they call upon the whole human being. And because the whole human is addressed, he can become more and more himself.

As everybody knows, living together is not easy. Ask any married couple. It only becomes possible through the conviction that problems are positive challenges which can further relationships and deepen them. Community life is healing when we decide to do this, when we do not run away from the people who make things hard for us, but take the opportunity to work the problem through. This means getting involved. In so doing a number of things can happen. More often than not we come face to face with our own prejudice and weakness. We also usually discover quite unsuspected secrets about the person, the one who was so difficult. We begin to see how he sees the world, what his hopes and dreams may be or his fears and doubts. This can happen with anyone, an ill child, a disturbed young person, one of our colleagues, any other human being with whom we have chosen to share our life and destiny. Because we chose in freedom, just as in a marriage, to live with this person, we are able to call upon something greater than ourselves to work into the relationship. We can call upon the higher being of the other as well as our own and allow both our lives to change.

The image of man is not static. Image is perhaps a misleading word because in fact the archetype of all life-bearing forms must include their existence in time. This we call biography. We have an outer biography and also an inner biography. As we progress from childhood through youth to the many further stages of life, we go from one world view to another and to another. At times our very personality may seem to change. So much can happen to one human between birth and death.

In choosing to live in a community with others, we chose to share life. This means sharing biography, being willing to accompany others through thick and thin. It means holding firmly to the faith that each person is more than the particular temporal manifestation we see before us. It means being convinced that although he may be living out his particular way of being as a child or a teenager or person who struggles with mid-life uncertainty, he is all the time trying to become the free individual that he really is. Surprising things can happen. The apparently hopeless teenager may become an outstanding adult; a backward child may develop later into a genius. Without extraordinary insight we can be easily deceived by the outer phenomena. We can form such a fixed picture of the other person that we help trap him in a stage of his biography. Only faithfulness to the true individuality within a changing picture helps him to avoid being trapped, and can allow him to *become*.

In a similar way metamorphosis is also a phenomenon of community biography. Members of a community need to have the same kind of faithfulness to the individuality of being of their community and its ideals as they should have to one another over the years. This is all the harder because communities include the complexities of many human beings all at different stages of development and with differing perceptions of the community itself. A community is born when a group of people begin to live and work together. They are few. There is little need to have formal meetings because they are always together. Soon they become an efficient organism, harmonious and radiant with the united intentions of those first pioneers. This young community attracts others. It doubles in size. The harmony, the intimacy is harder to achieve. Some feel left out. There are disagreements, opposite opinions. Now there is the need for more objective meeting grounds to reach consensus over community matters. In time these meeting spaces become part of the life-form of the place. They become habits. In the meantime more and more new people come. Some of the originals leave. The origin of the community forms and the ideals which once filled them is but a dim memory to most. Some begin to question and criticize. The community must undergo a kind of life crisis in order to find new forms appropriate to its age. And so on. Without the courage to change, to risk metamorphosis, sometimes at the very deepest levels, the community would cut itself off from its living spirit impulse. It would become an institution, automatic and dried up. The very effort of those living together to fight through again and again to the perception of the guiding impulse that brought them together can become the life-line to the image of man, the image of community.

The image of man stands always above each one of us, but each of us also has to suffer the trials of earthly life, our own illness, our own darkness or deformity, be it of body or soul or spirit. We need others to love not only what we want to become, but also to love who we are now, so that the illness can be healed, the darkness dispelled, the deformity understood. Such love is engendered by confidence in the positive working of destiny. Such love, if it lives in a community devoted to the needs of human beings, will ensure that its forms will always be flexible and evolve according to the many-sided humanity of those within it.

I said that I would try to describe why I came to Camphill and why I have stayed all these years. For me it was always connected with my growing understanding of the spiritual image of man and the community response to the needs of the individual. Such a response must grow out of human hearts infused by love which flows as a force of life from human being to human being.

A threefold image of man

Peter Roth

It is staggering how great a role money plays in our time. What an enormous amount of destiny hangs on how much money one actually earns! It is amazing to observe how events or movements, activities, use or misuse of human strength, waste or lack of emotions and empathy, subjective or objectively valid judgments, depend on and are determined by money. Starting in the fifteenth and sixteenth centuries, money became something in itself and had therefore the possibility of becoming a possession. Money has become the most powerful ally of materialism.

In the first months of Camphill's beginnings, new dimensions of work dawned on us, and with it the impossibility of salaries for work. The structure of our lives — living and working together with handicapped children; the fulfilment of the many necessities of life from cooking to being educated by Dr König to the celebration of the festivals — became so real to us that a reflected shadow of a corresponding salary structure seemed unreal. People should have what they need — food, clothing, books, cigarettes, holidays — not according to the amount of money they have; rather the community in which they work should make these things available to them, according to what the community has at its disposal. A good amount of talking, friendship and empathy is necessary to come to a real concept of "I need", particularly in relation to another person!

There are many consequences of not paying salaries. It touches the whole realm of possessions. You own the salary, and within its boundary you have the freedom to do with it what you like. But this is a sham freedom, a fool's paradise; you imagine what you can spend it on, and therefore you never get an idea of what you really need. Money — salary, capital in any form — *forces* you, potentially, to spend it. There is a danger that by having money you are led into a maze of needs, glamorous advertisements, status symbols and wish fulfilment that has very little to do with your destiny and real needs. Earthly possessions, money or any form of capital, are inclined to make earthly life seem a thing in itself, unrelated to spiritual existence, or anything beyond the purely material. Earthly possessions are an illusion; in biblical language, you cannot take your treasures to heaven. As the economy of our time is based on possessions, and we are all children of our time, our lives, with regard to their economic foundations, are not true. Camphill's estates do not belong to the co-workers, or the bearers of the Camphill impulse. Those who work in Camphill do not get a salary and personal possessions are few. Yet we are inevitably part of the economic life of our time.

We understood that an anthroposophical knowledge of man, of history and the world, gives rise to a particular social ordering that shows itself clearly in social organisms with handicapped children and adults. There are three separate realms. One of them is the economic; another the activities in the realm of ideas, for example education, or science; and the third is purely human. It therefore became clear to us that Marx — not only theoretically, but also existentially — was inconsequent in saying that all cultural, artistic and religious activity is only the smoke rising out of man's economic conditions. Marx built into his theory events which were not caused by *economic* changes, but by *human phenomena*. It was part of his theory that the employers had to stop being selfish, and the workers had to stop suffering. Violence and revolution were therefore part of the means to bring about this paradisal state. But exhorting sermons — religious or violent — belong to the past. The age of enlightenment has dawned; freedom lies in understanding.

We gradually became aware — and are still in the process of coming to understand — that a "salary-less" state of affairs is a first step to the "threefold social order" about which Rudolf

Steiner spoke frequently to many different audiences, and which he meant to be the foundation of any social organism.

Schumacher's *Small is Beautiful* seemed to us to formulate perfectly the concept for which our originally very small community had aimed: a kind of social laboratory for many different conditions. When you do not pay wages, the way is free for human relationships and friendships, beyond sympathy and antipathy. You must meet every human being as a person against whom violence and crime is not possible, and who demands a certain respect. That the other two realms I mentioned follow from this relationship to other people becomes clear if one considers that in the economic realm any work is only reasonable if it benefits others, and in the realm of ideas one must be free to utter one's own ideas and live out of them in relationship to others. A knowledge of Anthroposophy is by no means necessary to understand and experience these three principles. But it needs a group of committed people to promote them; to incarnate them. To *live* with them helps against what so many suffer today: alienation, inner loneliness, a gradual loss of identity, even sleeplessness. Self-doubt melts away if you are recognized as a person needed in the progression of the world

The experience of Camphill shows that the social organism can work in two ways: we must look *away* from ourselves in building up the social organism and must realize that we can become better, achieve a new stature, come nearer to our own selfless star, *through* the social organism.

The process towards trying to become more truly human which goes on in all Camphill centres with regard to the co-workers as well as the handicapped children, adolescents and adults, is due to this twofold stream — from social organism to the individual, and from the individual to the social organism: both benefit from each other.

The Bible evening in the village

Deborah Hudson

In each house community within the larger community we all meet together on Saturday evening and, held within the arms of the special Bible evening verses, share a meal and speak together. During the meal we try to have a more uplifted conversation, less to do with our opinions and more to do with seeking insights. When the meal is over we speak about a passage in the New Testament which we have thought about during the week. The evening begins with fifteen minutes sitting silently in a circle. This is the most basic description I can give of a Bible evening. It has this outer form and it has an inner reality. Yet a tremendous patience is needed to see and hear what really happens to us all on Saturday evening.

In preparing the Bible evening one has to be ready to tread a path of self-knowledge. The house cleaning and table setting are shared, and everything must be made to look as beautiful as possible. All the outward preparation demands a great deal from the individuals doing the work so that through their living involvement the Bible evening does not become either a tradition or a huge amount of hard work in which one feels no joy. We constantly fall between these attitudes and this tempts one time and again to give up. But when we do not give up we may have a particular experience. Perhaps we can experience the marriage of matter and spirit, as out of all the turbulence another dimension seems to arise.

At seven in the evening on Saturday, a bell sounds in Botton Village. It is meant to say, "All is prepared for Bible evening." In every house the table is set and the meal ready; everyone is waiting. If I walk through our house at this time something extraordinary happens. The air becomes a little denser and the house seems to answer us and our efforts by emanating a fragrance and an unearthly beauty and peace. This is the small moment in the week where, for not more than a few seconds, one can understand and experience that all our outer efforts make for a difference that is not just about outer cleanliness and tidiness. The house, and all in the house, takes on a deeper meaning. Life and matter ring out their significance again. If I walk about Botton at this time on a Saturday I can experience that the whole village has a special stillness. I am aware, in a very particular way, of the birds, the weather, the light, and the sound of the wind. It is as if I see everything for the first time . . . everything awaits the Bible evening, and something great does draw near.

When we meet together in silence before the meal we seem to approach a threshold; once again we must be prepared for self-knowledge. Two things can happen: our heads can buzz and our emotions press upon us, or we can experience stillness and refreshment from the well-spring in ourselves. The silence can be very nourishing if we can meet it properly.

The meal itself is often rather joyful. It is a meal where things look special: there is a white cloth and napkins, candles, special flowers, buns and honey. The food and the table itself are uplifted. We try and make a renewed effort towards each other during this meal and often we rediscover each other. The special Bible evening space leaves the possibility for these unobtrusive miracles.

After the meal we clear the table and sit while one of us reads aloud the passage from the New Testament. Then we speak about it. Often during the conversation one can find a truth one needs at that particular moment. In that setting one can experience who one's fellow human beings really are because very often in that specially prepared space we shine differently for each other.

I have written down some of the things I experience about the Bible evening. I must explain that it is an ideal we aspire to and in which we ever and again fail to achieve. We can be tired, we can rationalize and say there is no time, or we can just go to the cinema.

The Bible evening is the moment in the week where we make the transition from every-day to holy day. We have the chance to breath new inspiration into all aspects of our life. The individual takes on the seemingly impossible task of seeing the weekend approach after a busy week, and being asked not to do less but to do more. One is asked not to stop and relax but to make an effort to go beyond tiredness and "everydayness" and create an atmosphere were meaning can be found.

Living in Camphill involves a huge effort. There is a constant demand on us to change and make new efforts. Because nothing is insignificant one cannot say that this or that is not my problem. The Bible evening seems essential in this context. It is a still point where we can orientate ourselves again. It is a remembering of what lies behind our efforts. It is a very special statement of how we receive nourishment not by relaxing but by returning with renewed efforts to the well-spring.

Building blocks

Karin von Schilling

Part of the heritage of European culture that one occasionally comes across is a mighty cathedral. There it stands, in greater than human dimensions and formed out in thousandfold details in spires, pillars and statues. Who built such a cathedral? Who was the master builder? Who were the innumerable workmen and artists? Their selfless service was done for little remuneration, given for the glory of God and the use of people to come, and the fact that no names were added to their works adds spiritual value to the cathedral.

Camphill has been in existence for only a brief time compared with these great cathedrals. But one may still be led to make a comparison. The Camphill movement is not a spatial, geographically confined, physical building, and yet it has its specific structure, its earthly places and its significance in a specific century, the twentieth century. In this age — which struggles with the seeming polarities of individualization and community, of uniqueness and equality, with isolation and communes — a master builder and his co-workers attempted to create a structure in which people can live. Dr Karl König was the master. He created the master plan in terms of what one may call social architecture and his collaborators helped to bring it about in earthly reality. Today everybody can know of it. Its content is the Camphill Movement. To bring it about required the will for the good. It required "bricks and mortar" in human terms.

When some of us young people arrived in Camphill, Scotland, after the Second World War, we "became" the bricks. The mortar that kept us together was the needs of the very many severely handicapped children given into our care.

It is relatively easy to be enthusiastic about fine, futuristic images. But it was not comfortable being a brick! A brick has little opportunity to make advances on the road to self realization. It is placed were it is needed. Indeed that was the first demand: that specific likes or even gifts had to be sacrificed. Many of us shared our bedroom with a group of children — "our" children. One of the seven or eight beds in a dormitory was for one of us! I need not explain what a tall order that was for acquiring tidy habits and self discipline. Order is the firm base for everything spiritual. We worked where it was needed. We cleaned on hands and knees. It was customary that each one had to take over one of the big kitchens for at least one term, whether we had experience in cooking or not. It was an excellent but hard school in many respects and it taught us that one's security is not to be found in outer things, but only within. Endless examples could be given of how rigorously any possessiveness was curbed. We changed houses as the need arose, and that was often, for the first 15 years. Many of us, I dare say, had to forego dear wishes to move on to further enriching training places elsewhere. But we stayed on. We knew we were working to create a new culture in answer to a great need of our century. Rudolf Steiner put it into these words:

> The sacrifice of his own separate being,
> of his own life, the man must bring
> who will behold the spirit's purposes
> behind the senses' revelations;
> who dares to let the spirit's will
> stream down into his own.*

We had great examples, first and foremost in Dr König himself. His early successes promised a brilliant career as a doctor and researcher, yet he sacrificed this to forming a community, a movement, that grew slowly because it depended on the free will and individual growth of its members — its bricks. There were also his collaborators, his friends: Thomas Weihs, a gifted young doctor who spent seven years working on a small farm with delinquent boys; and a painter, Carlo Pietzner, who worked for years with severely spastic children, to name just two. Their real gifts matured greatly by giving this freely-willed sacrifice. All this was contained in the small word, work.

However, we were certainly not to drown in practical work! There were the other two basic needs: devotion and spiritual striving. The unique contribution that the master builder Dr König gave us was the introduction of social forms. Without them nothing would have been achieved, even if each "brick" had been aglow with warmth and good will we would have remained a pile of bricks! One of Camphill's greatest contributions is to allow individuals to grow mutually in social encounter. This requires *form*. Three social forms were introduced and practised. They grew out of the needs of our everyday lives and appear directed to the work in our schools and villages with handicapped people. However, if one has lived with

* From *The Soul's Probation*, Scene 7. In *The Four Mystery Plays*, translated by Adam Bittleston.

them one recognizes their value far beyond their present use in our places. They are: the discipline of the college meeting; the Bible evening; and the implementation of the Fundamental Social Law as formulated by Rudolf Steiner.*

The Fundamental Social Law crystallized for us the aim of not claiming the proceeds of our labour for ourselves. Outwardly this was applied in terms of a no-wage agreement, thus it pertained to the economic sphere of human life. But our whole life was coloured by it, including the interpersonal human sphere and the cultural life. This led to the continuous effort to be willing to pass on to others what one might have gathered as achievements or expertise. The first group of pioneers gave us a shining example of this and it culminated outwardly in their willingness to pass on the leadership responsibilities to groups of younger people. These "older" people were in their late thirties; and we were in our twenties! This sacrifice was hard for them too, but it made the growth of the world-wide Camphill movement possible.

The three basic conditions — work, devotion and spiritual striving — permeated the three social forms: the college meeting, the Bible evening and the endeavour to implement Rudolf Steiner's Fundamental Social Law. Through such striving each person could forge an armour that resisted the temptation to spiritual arrogance and prevented us from losing sight of the essentially Christian message of Anthroposophy.

It is impressive to look at the manifestations of the Camphill movement, but I believe the key to its further growth will live with each individual who is prepared to allow his life to be governed by the three "building" disciplines as described above, for inherent in them are the words of Rudolf Steiner quoted above. The intent to do this can only be born in individuals who wish to counter the overwhelming social problems of our time with the recognition that Goethe put into words: "One alone can do little, but if one joins others at the right time much can be done."

My hope is that coming generations of co-workers will not feel frustrated or shackled by the weight of what has been achieved in the first fifty years. I hope that they will accept this heritage and realize that their searching gaze must look higher into other areas of need where work, devotion and spiritual striving may be applied. May they continue to join hands with the many who have striven to overcome powers . . . not in flesh and blood, but in high places (in the words of St Paul) so that the healing will of Christ may prevail.

The Christianizing of the earth

Christoph Jensen

One does not have to be a jetsetter to experience just how much our globe has shrunk, in distance as well as in customs, attitudes, pursuits, education and, ultimately, thinking. Bound to cities as most people are, there is not much difference in entering an office or department store in Helsinki, Manchester, Chicago or Cape Town. What is different is the climate, although in a city this is hardly noticeable, provided it is not subject to a heatwave, snowstorm or hurricane. It is as if in the past forty or fifty years an equalizing force has come over our earth which makes us more and more aware of our common humanity. In its wake it might have brought a lamentable loss of regional, perhaps national, identity, but certainly — and this process has not finished — it has also brought us an ability to identify with others in a way never before possible.

This regional or national identity was expressed in what we commonly call folklore. Sharing this folklore enriches the lives of countless others in that they can enjoy expressions of soul they were not aware of before. Folklore was freed for the sake of humanity's lore; a tapestry

* See Barbara Lipsker's contribution earlier in this chapter.

is woven of soul expressions and put on exhibition at folk festivals, carnivals or the cultural history museums. Freed from his particular folklore, man begins to experience himself as *man*. Instead of sympathy and antipathy, something new arises in the souls of men: empathy.

These soul expressions were in the widest sense part of the nature of the different peoples, part of their habitat, which, of course, was largely rural. To the extent that man left and leaves the rural areas and becomes a citizen of the world, he also takes leave of habits, customs and traditions imposed on him by his natural surroundings. We are witnesses to a fascinating revolution, but there has been a price to pay. This price is the agony of witnessing the suffering of nature, nay, the suffering of the earth. I do not have to go into detail describing the destruction and desertification of a once blooming countryside. The decay has set in. But what is it that we behold? Is it not that we recognize the earth as a being in its own right, as much as plants, animals and men are beings in their own right?

For many of the co-workers it was the villagers who led them from the city to the rural areas, into the Camphill villages. And in the villages we experience that what is regarded as therapy for man is simultaneously an act of healing for the earth. With the celebration of the festivals, the naming and dedication of the fields, the laying out of the gardens, and, of course, the rhythmic work with the seasons and plants, and the daily routine with the animals, we found areas considered wasteland springing to life. With the building of houses, chapels, halls, roads and footpaths, we are acutely aware that we are creating and permeating landscapes. Socializing suddenly attains another meaning apart from its bourgeois connotations. It is the sociability of the person so aptly called the villager who leads us there.

The healing of the earth will succeed to the extent that we understand each other to be landscape gardeners, because for good or bad this is what we are engaged in: landscape gardening. The wasteland we see around us is largely a result of our thoughtlessness. The landscapes of old are gone, as much as the old social forms. The landscapes of the future will be a reflection of the ways we are able to live with and relate to each other.

It was Mary Magdalene who, meeting the Christ at the tomb, thought he was the gardener. By being truly interested in one another, we can free others from their tombs of loneliness, selfishness and thoughtlessness, and thereby make space for their creativity.

Vladimir Soloviev, in an essay on the work of man for the earth, says:

Man's relation to nature is of three kinds: passive submission to it; subjugating it and merely employing it as a means to an end; the affirmation of nature's ideal potential state, of what it ought to become through the activity of man. Absolutely moral and final is the third relationship, in which man uses his efforts for the sake of uplifting nature, and uplifts himself along with it.*

How then are we going to uplift nature? I suggest it shows in the effort of taking such a statement literally: namely, to uplift the mundane, that which we take for granted, like placing the toothpaste tube on a saucer, laying a table neatly, keeping order in one's timetable, dusting and airing the stuffy corners of our existence. In other words, where we have become animals of habit, to change into humans with a purpose and an attitude. Human dignity comes with order, and order is uplifting. No matter how high our ideals, they stand or fall when we try to put them into practice. Rudolf Steiner spoke to curative teachers about a new religious attitude and referred to "the devotion to the small things" in life; it is the charity that begins at home.

The uplifting of nature is practised by the farmer when he ploughs as much as when we sit around a table at Bible evening with a lit candle and thereby raise the level of conversation. When we speak about apocalyptic times, don't we refer to chaos, to a social wasteland? But are we aware that apocalypse means as much the beginning as it does the end; a beginning through grace? Grace is inseparable from humility. And if we humble ourselves enough we may well be able to accept our villagers as being our teachers.

* "Justification of the Good," in Natalie Duddington, *The Religious Philosophy of Soloviev*, Hibbert Journal, Boston 1917, Vol.5.

Our world can do with a lot of re-creation — by re-creating we add the human touch to things mechanical. Two people can do the same thing, the one out of habit, the other with enthusiasm, out of submission or re-creation, asleep or awake. These are the choices before all of us, villager and co-worker alike. Life needs a sparkle. I believe the sparkle to be Christianity. This also needs re-creation; the opportunity to apply the sparkle is manifold. Hidden within each one of us, it wants to unite with what was God's creation.

Chapter 4

Life extracts

Camphill villages: a way of life*

There is a wooded, quiet valley in rural upstate New York. There are some old red barns, cows graze in the outlying meadows, and a brook runs through the valley. A peace-drenched, seemingly forgotten place, it is the home of Camphill Village. When you enter this village in the valley, you enter a certain timelessness.

In the heart of the village, glowing red through the trees, stands a strikingly faceted, thoroughly modern building: Fountain Hall. Below it lies the hall pond, quietly reflecting the ever changing village life. In spring, this is the place to catch the first signs of new life: squirming tadpoles and salamanders. In the summer there are picnics, games, folk dancing, and cacophonous bullfrog choruses. In autumn it gathers wind-blown russet leaves, and in winter it hums with skaters.

Fountain Hall is the gathering place for this village community. Its vaulted interior hosts cultural, artistic, educational and social activities. The village assembles here to celebrate a festival, a wedding, a special birthday. Musical gifts are shared through concerts, choirs and speech choruses which resound within its walls. Sometimes guest performers entertain. Plays, skits and pageants are performed, and it is a place for meetings, lectures and common study. The community gathers here for worship. Like rays from this centre, footpaths reach through the woods, over the brook, past fields, across the road, uphill and down, leading to neighbourhoods of houses, the old barn, the new farm complex, craft shops, co-op store and garden. Within this landscape more than two hundred people live together in a therapeutic community. About half are mentally handicapped adults.

Come, choose a path, walk down it and enter this landscape. How soon someone comes to meet you. Come, take a tour. Your guide greets you with an ear-reaching grin, an energetic and prolonged handshake, and bubbling vivacity. She seems proud that you have come to see her village. The way she talks, you might think she owned the place. And in a way, she does.

Along the way, you pass a tall, determined, rather elegant man intently guiding a profoundly handicapped woman down the country road. Suddenly, he drops her hand, spins around three times, bends down, picks up a leaf and crumples it between his fingers. He sniffs it, gingerly, then goes back to fetch his charge and proceeds with renewed determination. You meet many people on the way to work, and they check your progress repeatedly.

"Who are you?"

"Nice day!"

"You happy?"

"It's my birthday tomorrow."

"You like it here?"

There is openness, friendliness and warmth.

Climb the hill to the Birchtree workshops, a high, light, modern complex of three craft shops. First you go to the candle shop; such fragrant peace reigns there. Some workers carefully dip candles, others sit around a table polishing, trimming and packing them. Then you come to the book bindery, an airy and calm shop full of quiet industry and concentration. People

* This contribution originally appeared in *Village Life*, edited by Cornelius Pietzner, Neugebauer Press, 1986.

Murtle estate sports centre

are cutting, folding, sewing, gluing. There is a pile of handmade books covered in fabric woven or batiked in the village. The enamel shop is next. The room is painted a bold fuchsia, and hanging plants bloom in the window. Here sits our pirouetting friend, calmly polishing copper. Others are involved in the various stages of enamelling. The work-master gets down from his bench to greet you. There are some finished products on display, bowls and platters with transparent, flowing colours and forms. What unexpected beauty!

"Come along," your guide suggests, "there's much more to see!"

You meet a baker along the road who is still aproned and capped in white, carrying a bright blue bucket of fresh loaves. Someone else approaches, does not stop or even raise his head, but only continues on slowly, buried in solitude. An officious looking gentleman passes. He nods rather curtly, checks his timepiece, and moves right along with his attache case under his arm. An inspector? No, he is the village courier, delivering internal mail and messages.

Do you hear that loud "Ya-a-Hoo-o-!" echoing down in the valley? The farmers are bringing in the cows from pasture. One farmer wears an unusual three-cornered hat — his T-shirt — wrapped around his head. The other has a broad, contagious grin. If you follow their footsteps, you would come to Sunny Valley barn where you could watch them hand-milk their cows.

Here come the gardeners; their wheelbarrows overflow with spinach and onions. One stops, picks up a basket of vegetables and carries it into the house. He wipes his muddy boots, hastily, and proceeds through the boot-room inside. Would you like to go inside too?

You wander into the living-dining room. There is a round wooden table set for twelve with a vase of fresh flowers in the centre on a hand-woven cloth. The window-sills are filled with plants and crystals. Original artwork adorns the walls. Your guide pops into the kitchen.

"Hi," she says. "How was my soup this morning? Did you like it? What are you making for supper?" And then to you: "I work here in the mornings and today I made borscht. Here is my work-master." You meet the housemother with a crew of helpers. They might be preparing supper, making jam, churning cream into butter, or beginning to process the newly-delivered basket of vegetables. Someone may be cleaning out closets, ironing, or mending.

"Well," your guide says, "I've got to go back to my workplace. They need me now. It was a pleasure to meet you."

If you had really taken a tour of the village, your guide would have made sure you had also seen the wood-shop, the doll-shop, the bakery, the weaving shop, and the garden. You

72

would have been reminded to stop at the gift shop on your way out of the village. Indeed, you would have been invited into a village house, where you would have been received by a housemother, offered refreshments and the opportunity to ask some of your questions:

"What is this place, what is Camphill?"

"What are you doing?"

"How do you do it?"

"For whom?"

"Why?"

Wanda Root, Camphill Village, New York, has been a co-worker in England and America for many years.

About workshops

Once in a while a special occasion comes around. When Camphill first started it was very special for Karl König, as he had left the war behind and was able to focus his particular talents on a new peace. Those of us who now live in Camphill may well give pause, and endeavour to think where we might be if Camphill had not been started. In many ways what I write now is but a "thank-you" from all Camphill dwellers for the existence of Camphill.

When I first started to work in the pottery, at the start and end of the day I would meet people who were going to the woodwork shop or weavery and so just in that short meeting of maybe five minutes we found a common identity, a common ground; we had become one of a kind. I personally find it very tricky to separate workshops from the farm and garden, now that I come to think about it. People go to work in the farm and garden just as much as they do in the workshops. Many a time the people in the workshops have been asked to give a hand with the harvesting or fruit picking, and it is nice to meet people we live with when they are in their own element. More often than not I have been working in the pottery and I

Glass engraving, Botton Village

73

*Work and rest at bakeries
in Beitenwil (above) and
Botton (right and below).*

have had visitors from the farm and garden and heard them comment on the skill required to make or throw a pot.

Do I find it common-place to have our own vegetables? No, I personally find it pretty special. I suppose what I am trying to say is that it really does not matter what we do as long as we do it. So now comes that distinction between what we do, and what we do well. Many people would probably not believe that they possess special talents. I know when I first met pottery I was happy to do almost anything because I found the pottery, or "place of work" a nice place to be in. I was fascinated by the wheel and showed enough interest to have a try.

I met workshops as a whole before I met pottery. When I first came to Camphill it was in Glencraig and it was so that a newcomer had a week in a workshop and the next week in another workshop. This was to try and find where a person would be most happy. I found this in itself pretty special because it is not so often you like your work. As a rule work was just somewhere you were put and you did this job or you were "out". This was a great pity because it is so that your work can be the ruling factor in a content life. Spend the day from 9 to 5:30 doing something that is not to your liking — many people either quit or it becomes automatic to them; the one is as detrimental as the other.

When people take their time to find out what work you are happy with, then something happens. A challenge comes around. I think many people find this to be the case. A job which was just a job becomes something more. We tried to make a better job out of an ordinary run-of-the-mill job, and that was because the effort was appreciated. This is very much an important point and probably the point at which work becomes important. The challenge to do a job of work well is appreciated, not only by the person who does it, but also by the person who asked for the job to be done.

When I first went to work in the pottery I noticed that care was taken in the work you were given. At first you were given a job that was well within your capabilities. As you progressed and you were having success the jobs were subsequently more difficult. There came a time when the choice of work was left to you. I think this was quite a testing time because it was assumed that you had been taught enough and therefore your proficiency was enough to let you get on with things, without instructions! This state of affairs can be very nice but, oh, it isn't nice when you are simply told to do twenty mugs followed by thirty candle-holders . . . ! The point being, I suppose: "Get good enough, and your responsibility goes up by half."

I think the main difference between farm and workshop is the small amount of space between you and your fellow workers. Tolerance is the key word! There is no space to walk away from whoever, because Monday is treating them wrongly. However, remember your own imperfections and take into account that your neighbour might well have a headache and you are half-way there. What we must remember is that by going to our day's work we have proven to ourselves that we are capable, and capability is a very important factor to all of us.

John Porten, a villager in Hapstead, Devon.

News from the bakery

I started to work in the bakery just before Christmas. Michael Balcombe used to be the baker, but he decided that he wanted to do something else. He had been the Grange-Oaklands baker for a number of years. Then Norman came to take over the bakery and Michael has been showing Norman the ropes. I must say it was nice watching Michael teaching and showing Norman what was done in the bakery. In the bakery there are several other people besides myself working. Angela, Andrew, Karl and Susanna work in the bakery in the mornings, also not forgetting Norman.

They start at around 7 o'clock in the morning or even earlier when Norman or Susanna light the ovens and start doing the dough. When it is about 8.30 then the bakery gets into full swing, busy making granary rye, honey salt, white bread, rolls, wholemeal or whatever is needed on that particular day. On Mondays a member of the bakery cleans the hall ready for the service, but then on Tuesday afternoon I can be seen delivering bread around the Grange and also at the end of the day. We put Oaklands' bread on the transport. Each week we pack Thornbury and Cherry Orchards, which are other Camphill places. We make special bread for festivals and also for the service (white). We have had increased orders from houses which means we have been very busy trying to meet people's needs.

Some people from outside have been buying our bread which is very nice indeed. I just thought I would write the prayer which the bakers say at the end of the day. One very nice thing is that visitors have commented on the bread and how nice it is.

Prayer of the Bread
O Raphael be our helper
By thy power of healing
Restore this weakened grain
May the power of the sun
Be in the gold of the crust
May the power of the air
Be in the rising of the leaven
May the warmth of our love
Add strength to the loaf

I'm afraid I don't know who wrote this prayer, perhaps the person wishes to be nameless. Norman and his happy band of bakers wish you happy eating and if there are any questions, please ask. Barbara is making new bread bags as the other ones are getting too old or are too small for the bread.

Thank you, Barbara, for making the bags.

Sue Donat, a villager, has been at Grange-Oaklands for the past ten years.

Baking in a Camphill community

Baking bread is a very responsible job for our everyday consumption within the community. The whole process of baking begins with weighing flour, adding salt, water and yeast and then comes the mixing of the ingredients in a bowl. Now comes the kneading process which transforms the whole mixture into dough (gluten). We press with all our strength using the palms of our hands and when the dough becomes lighter and bounces back when we touch it, it means it is ready. Then we put the dough in a bowl to let it rise and then we cut it into loaves. We knead the loaves and put them in tins to rise for a while, then we put them in the oven to bake for forty-five minutes, then we take them out and there we have our finished product.

Andrew Graham, a villager in Grange-Oaklands.

From my days in Grange pottery

There had been a crew of four to six villagers who had stayed with me in the slow and hard learning process in the craft of pottery. In the course of many years some of them had achieved a good overall skill and a consciousness for the whole complicated, manifold working process. In this way a very good co-operation had developed between us resulting in a considerable production of great variety.

The time of the year passed in the rhythmical change between feverish work and more relaxed periods when it was possible to deepen and perfect abilities and to practise new ones.

It began straight after the summer months with the strong push towards the Christmas sales which started in October, the conclusion of which was our Advent sale in the Grange. The other activities could stand in the foreground — no more rush till after the Holy Nights. There followed a time of steady production which filled our storeroom to its utmost capacity so that we were wondering where to put the next lot that came out of the kiln. But then the shops began to stock up for the summer business. Newton Dee craft-shop was one of our best customers. It was a relief to see everything disappear as it always did.

There was usually a happy, often hilarious atmosphere in the workshop. And indeed there were some unforgettable characters among us. Michael was the ever beaming sunshine of the place, sometimes with priceless remarks which, however, are difficult to relate to people not knowing him. Sometimes I was startled hearing a lengthy conversation going on next to me between John Canning and Innes Foley, co-workers supposed to be on business elsewhere, but it was only Jeremy who, bent over his work, in a one-man show, imitated the voices of these two gentlemen holding forth about the state and treatment of Grange motor cars or other subjects, in an absolutely perfect way. Or there came suddenly the many noises of a whole flock of sheep, big and small, interrupted by the neighing of a horse, the mooing of a cow and the penetrating shriek of a circular saw, all produced by the voice of A.R.L. with an incredible genuineness. It was the same A.R.L. who gave to our products the characteristic touch with his astonishing variety of beautifully executed engravings on mugs, dishes, jars and bowls. There was also gentle, friendly Ben with his wonderful care. He often came over after supper to take things out of the moulds or to cover them up to prevent them from getting too dry overnight. Never would he let any of his products perish, in contrast to Mary, who never remembered what had to be done with things coming off the wheel. And there was the faithful Sylvia who I knew from her school days at Newton Dee. She thrived in this company of originals, until after ten years she wanted a change and went to Botton.

So life went on in the pottery for twenty years. Some of the dear old friends left, but some remained steadfast. It was they who made it possible for the workshop to carry on even when I was finally called away, and a succession of different people took over the pottery with more or less knowledge of the craft — but the faithful potters were there to tide over. This, I think, is the greatest credit to them and deserves to be mentioned when we look back at the development of Camphill.

Erika Opitz, craft-master, Grange-Oaklands.

A day in the life of Beannachar garden

"Morning! Me again! Keep on going, don't stop!" Dominic is obviously ready for work this morning. I find him a large space where he can dig to his heart's content and return to the garden shed where others, less industrious, are slowly gathering. A small group settles down to string the onions into skeins of golden globes to hang under the rafters for winter. The sun shines and the work goes easily, one to rub off the dirt, one to sort out the good from the bad, one to twist the skeins among the string.

I take a group to clean a weedy patch of ground ready for autumn sown broad beans. "Alan," I say to a reluctant teenager, "could you bring a barrow for the weeds?" Alan turns

Haymaking (above) and gathering straw bales (opposite) at Botton Village.

his back and runs out of the garden. "Alan! ALAN!!" Sounds of stampeding feet beyond the garden wall. Some minutes later he reappears, grinning apologetically, wheeling a squeaky wheelbarrow.

Two heads of hennaed hair move above the beans and rounding the corner two ex-co-workers drift into view. "We are here for a few days. Can we do anything?" In the greenhouse juicy red tomatoes are falling off the vines, and beside the path french beans grow longer and tougher. It is good to have a few extra pairs of hands.

The lunch bell goes and everyone downs tools. Some only too literally — a fork flies into the bushes, a hoe is dropped into the weeds. These retrieved, we troop in to remove welly boots and wash hands.

The afternoon begins. The cook, wearied after his morning's labours, wanders out hoping for a quiet moment. Another co-worker, whose love is any machinery but especially the tractor, takes an enthusiastic group whooping with joy off down the drive to collect leaves for compost and branches for sawing. Everything has settled down nicely with no mishaps, except that Kylan has fallen into the flower bed again. A lorry laden with straw roars up the drive followed a few minutes later by an excited group of leaf rakers. Everyone rushes round to the farm and bales of straw are passed from hand to eager hand. Most of it ends up in the barn safely under cover, but a few broken bales remain to litter the yard and are swept up by conscientious hands. The rest of us return to the garden. Half an hour before supper, what shall we do?

Some return quite happily to their jobs and peace reigns again. Others, less settled, help to gather vegetables and deliver them to the store ready for the cooks tomorrow.

"Hard work! Hard work!" puffs one, laden under a full basket of leeks, their green leaves trailing like seaweed around his shoulders and under his arms.

Yes, it is hard work, but when the day's work is done and we troop in for supper we can stretch our feet under the laden table and feel a good day's work has been done.

Celia Baldwin, Beannachar.

78

A work-day

I have a very good working order. In Newton Dee village I think many people do. My name's Raymond Friskney, rather a strange surname isn't it? There's so few people with such a surname. I come from Grimsby town — a fishing port. It was a major fishing port at one time.

My work, like most villagers except for the farmers and bakers, begins at nine o'clock. We usually have breakfast at eight o'clock in Orion where I live, and have lived for over fifteen and a half years. I just won't leave Orion; I like it very much. In Orion we have seven other people: Pamela Watkins, Peter Mason, Helmella, Emma Jackson and Susan Furth who's been in Camphill centres since she was a child. We have a child living with us, and Irene.

I work in the store with Vitus and Valerie Werthmann who are in charge, and Martin Harris, their right-hand man, Guy Sproat, the shadow boss, John Blanchard and Mark Hughs and Viola, a young German co-worker who is with us for a year. We make up orders for the schools and the village and have lots of outside customers.

Work stops at 12 o'clock and then I return to Orion for lunch and help to set the lunch table.

In the afternoon I work in the laundry with Simon Blaxland de Lange in charge, and a co-worker called Gerlinde who lives in Roadside Cottage. The rest of the team are as follows: Ingrid Hughs who also has a sister called Margarete who lives in Capella with Valerie and Vitus; Eleanor, who lives in Morven; Tony Pitman, who lives with Simon in Lyra; Pamela Watkins, who lives with me in Orion; Audrey Rae, who lives in the farm. Sometimes Flora MacFarlane, who's also in Lyra with Simon and Tony. We have a young man from Murtle called Alexander who does the folding and works on the spin drier filling it up.

Various people deal with different parts of the laundry work. Most people can fold the sheets, table clothes and duvet covers and pillowcases, but the ironing is usually done by a few people: Ingrid, Eleanor, Pam, Gerlinde, Simon and myself. Pamela does most of the finishing touches and puts the laundry on to the various shelves where it goes.

79

We pack the laundry on Friday mornings and deliver it to the Camphill School estates in the afternoon.

So that's my work routine for the week and we have talks and other activities. In the evenings I mainly read maps and novels.

Raymond Friskney, a villager at Newton Dee.

"Oh, good and bad, good and bad"

I suppose it all happened on the twenty-sixth of December 1961, that I, as a rather nervous new villager entered Botton for the first time and the start of a new life, so totally different to — and to have a profound change on — what had been my life up to then.

Some months before, I had gone to Harley Street to be interviewed by Thomas Weihs and it had been agreed that I would go for a trial holiday of two weeks. The only thing was that "two weeks" has turned into some twenty-eight years that I have been associated with Camphill, a thing I had no idea of at the time, nor do I suspect did the many long-suffering co-workers and teachers that it has been my good fortune to meet both now and then. Perhaps twenty-eight years is rather a long "trial holiday"!

So there I was at the threshold of a new life, which up till then had been pretty pointless, now to be met by not only a point to my life, but a challenge, as I felt deep within my inner being called upon to a realization of an acknowledgement of my higher being, for whether in the cultural life, work life, or just on the daily contact of being a true human being, I was met by true human understanding.

Not that my early days at Botton were easy, far from it as I had to come to grips with the mirror reflection that was Michael Parker which, as I say, was no easy task, but still the many co-workers I came into contact with held up that mirror and said: "If you cannot accept the

Blessings on the meal

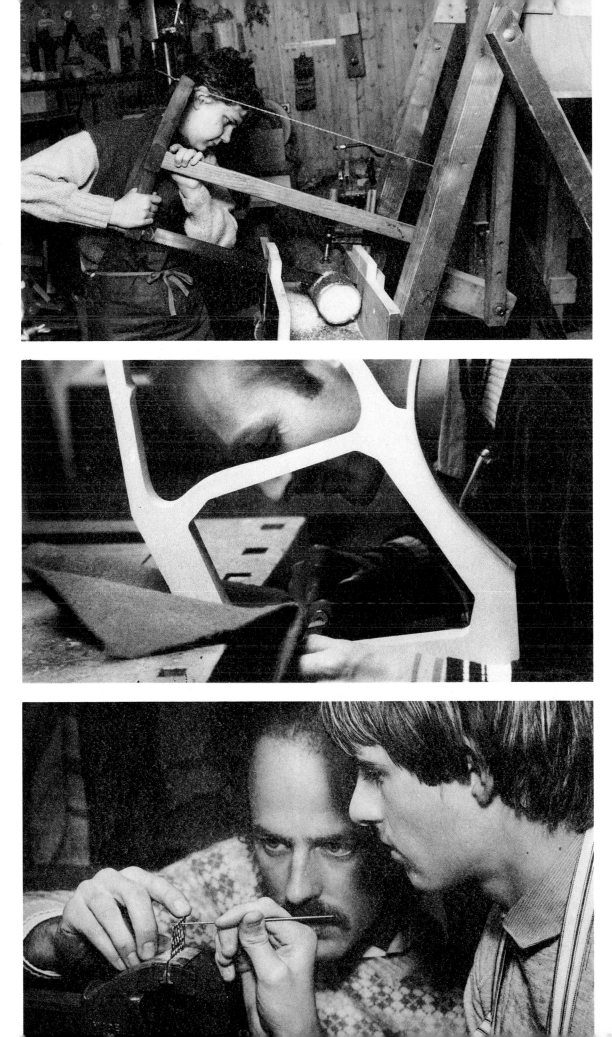

Training and craft workshops make musical instruments and metalwork.

image that is cast there, change it, don't just sit around and bemoan your fate, do something about it." And so, by degrees, and with the help of the whole of Camphill, I was able to change it, I hope, for the process is still going on, some twenty-eight years later.

It may be wondered what has made the most impression on me out of my association with Camphill. It is the work routine, or perhaps the plays that celebrate the Christian year, or just the community life that is led in school, village training centre, or half-way house (all of which I have had some experience of at one time or another within Camphill). It is none of these and yet it is all of them, for the one thing that I carry with me always is the one thing that embraces them all, namely that which makes Camphill unique, the Bible evening, for there we are occasionally privileged to see behind the veil, and to have a glimpse of the Spirit realm as man stands out as what he is supposed to be, and through him we are able to experience the finger of God as it writes on the hearts and souls of those present, be they villager or co-worker, or like me, just a guest. And one sees over and again the pulsating heart of Camphill beating to the eternal rhythm, and the life of the community starts to make sense, as one participates in the ever-renewing wonder, and you know that you are part of the whole, part of the community.

It can again be wondered why I have called these reflections of life in Camphill: "Oh, good and bad." That's soon told.

It was the first time that I met Dr König, and that was back in February 1962 after he had given a lecture at Botton on the special constellation that had occurred at that time in connection with the thalidomide child. I was introduced to him as a new villager, by Peter Roth, and he said: "Ah, so you are the Michael Parker I have heard so much about," to which I replied, "Only good things, I hope Herr Doctor." He just simply said: "Oh, good and bad, good and bad."

Farm-work and doll-making at Botton Village.

Well, all I can say is as I look back now on my association with Camphill, there have been far more good than bad memories that I carry with me. I look at the one-time little community

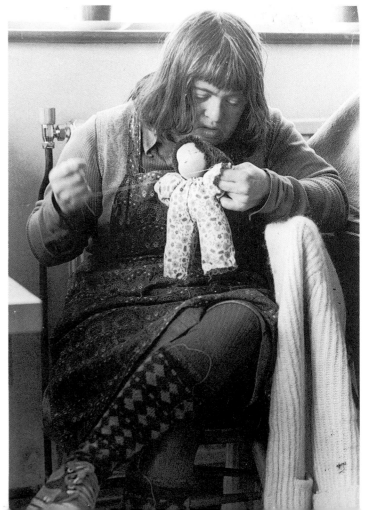

82

that now bestrides the globe like some great colossus, as Camphill has come to embrace many countries, creeds and cultures. This must surely be its true memorial, as friends and well-wishers celebrate its Golden Jubilee, and help it on into the twenty-first century, and beyond.

Michael Parker, a villager at Botton.

An outing

The climb to the Scottish castle had been strenuous, and we let Alice, our 52–year-old Down's friend, rest on a chair we found outside the locked ticket office. As it was midday the office was not manned, and we proceeded to climb the tower of the ruined castle. When we reached the top and looked down, we saw Alice looking with a smile on her face at the shining coins in her hand. We wondered what had happened and then saw another group of tourists who had arrived after us and given their £1 entry fee to our would-be ticket lady. Alice transferred the money to her pocket with a friendly "thank you".

Axel Stutz

A discovery

A short time ago I made a discovery — I noticed that the children living in my parents' house are handicapped. Looking back into childhood, I see children and adults living in my parents' house. I was a child and belonged to the world of children. We had our do's and don'ts, our likes and dislikes. We climbed trees together, roamed the world together, fought and had fun together.

Spinning and carding wool.

At nine and a half I went to boarding school. My school friends changed, but we were still children in a children's world. I do not remember them as being different to the children at home. As I grew older I started to baby-sit and then housekeep at home, the typical lot of the eldest child. At some point I must have registered intellectually that I was "different". But I have never quite known "different" to whom or what? I have always been me.

I went on to train and work as a social worker and eventually returned to work in Camphill. This summer I spent some days in my parents' house, my childhood home, and was surprised to see just how handicapped the children are who live there.

I asked my mother: "Were the children I grew up with in our house as handicapped as these children?" She looked at me and smiled, full of amusement at my perplexity, and said: "Yes, dear."

Veronica Hansmann was born and raised in Camphill and now works in Blair Drummond, Scotland.

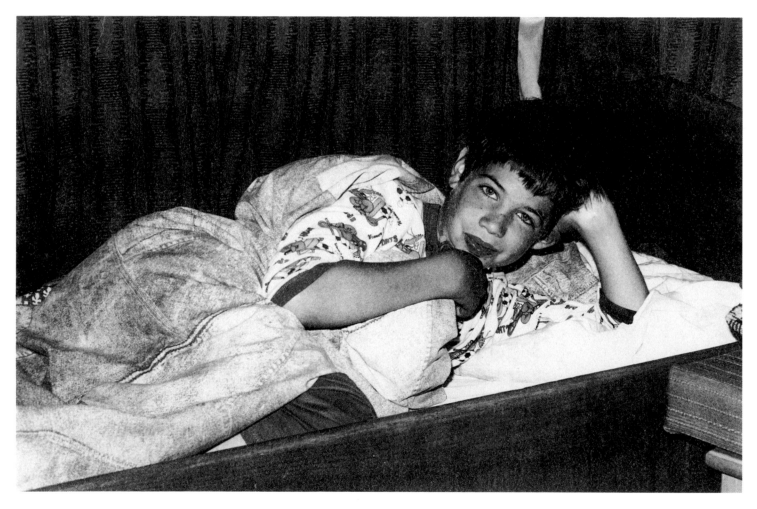

The way of my brother

My brother, Jonathan Gitlin, arrived on October 5, 1956, plunking himself down in New Rochelle, New York, in the midst of our family: my stepfather Harry Gitlin, my mother June, and my older sister Cathy.

Jon's birth was surrounded by a lot of confusion. There were tests, conferences, talking with doctors. We were finally told that Jon was a Down's syndrome baby, somehow different from the rest of us. This confusion didn't end with the diagnosis. A lot of questions remained to be answered: Was he truly? Wasn't he? How severely? How mildly? I was in the fifth grade, and these questions intruded into my life, which was filled with the politics of the school-yard and with finding the most appropriate way to drive our teacher out of her mind.

In the first year or so of Jon's life things seemed rather normal to me. I loved having a baby brother, and he seemed happy to be there. I would take him with me in a stroller when I went on errands, carry him piggyback for shorter distances, or around shops and stores, go to the zoo, watch him in the yard. There were other baby brothers around the neighbourhood, and Jon wasn't very different from the rest.

But, by the time he was two, it was clear that Jon was different. He had stayed a "baby" brother far longer than the brothers of my friends; he had stayed in the stroller for many months longer. He needed things done for him much longer. He didn't learn to walk well. He didn't speak so well. People wanted to know "what was wrong with him". Things didn't stay so "ordinary". To find my place, I had to change. I had to learn a new way.

Jon taught me. We began with patience, which he taught in a simple and pragmatic way. His reaction to adversity was to SIT DOWN. Immediately. Wherever he was. Completely boneless, limp. He would just flop down. And in that position he was a dead weight, far too heavy for me or anyone else to lift. This smiling baby brother, who five minutes before I had been carrying on my back, was now as ponderously heavy as the Rock of Gibraltar, and as impossible to move. My strength could not lift him. Cleverness was wasted on his resistance. It took patience, love, comfort and understanding (and a sense of humour) in strong doses, to transform him back to a manageable weight.

Jon taught me to see others in a clearer light. He was my barometer. Jon evoked a reaction from everyone. Nobody was immune. And these reactions revealed each person's character. He was slow to develop, and behind his age group physically, verbally, and in independence. Even at five and six he had to be pushed in his stroller, and couldn't express himself in a manner which was recognized as "normal". No-one escaped reacting to him, even if only for a fleeting moment. And in that reaction each person's psyche was revealed, and nothing done afterward could change the truth of that vision.

I began to decide certain things based on those reactions: I wouldn't shop at certain stores, because the owners' reactions to Jon were not kind or understanding. I judged the adults around me in the manner in which they related to Jon. Some patronized him, although at the time I would have said they just acted stupidly, and couldn't communicate with him directly.

But there were those who just accepted him and loved him simply. Jon's grandmother was one. A Russian Jewish immigrant, she had no notion of Down's syndrome; what it meant, the genetic truths which underlie it, or Jon's future. She just loved him and took care of him, just as she did the rest of her grandchildren. She has a permanent place in my heart, not just for this, but for this as much as anything. Our brother Sam, the youngest of the family, accepted him. As Sam quickly outraced Jon and surpassed him in physical and mental development, he quickly shifted gears and became the protector and older brother.

Still, Jon was an outcast. The society in which he found himself had no place for him. His behaviour was disquieting, his abilities too limited for him to find a comfortable place in state school or in special education classes. Our mother did yeoman's work. New Rochelle, where we lived, had not lived up to the laws of New York State which mandated the specifics of special education for children like Jonathan. So began the battle of the Board of Education. My mother, always a fighter, devoted herself to eliciting, by whatever means necessary, a proper compliance from the local authorities. Day after day, week after week, she fought with them; by letters to Albany and Washington, by letters to her legislators, and finally, by the most powerful means possible, learnt from Jon himself. She sat. In the waiting room of the superintendent of the Board of Education. Immovable. Knitting and sewing, reading and just waiting. Day after day, from the moment they opened until the moment they closed. Until finally they agreed to see her and fulfil their obligations.

Even so, Jon had not found his right place. He had helped to make sure that many children like him would be properly cared for in the state education system, but it wasn't his place.

And then a small article appeared in a local paper. Word was passed from parent to parent. A lecture was going to be given on disabled children — no, it was always "retarded children" — and on Camphill Special School, this "place" in Pennsylvania where everything was different. It could have been a notice for the appearance of Peter Pan, or an invitation to Never Never Land; it grabbed the attention of a number of parents who had been searching. They went to listen, and sat spellbound. It was Carlo Pietzner who then appeared. From that moment there was no question in my mother's mind as to where Jon should go. Interviews were set up. Carlo sat in a motel room and interviewed, not the parents, but the children. He had long and meaningful conversations with Jon, and with a number of other special children. A decision was made. They would go to Camphill.

Jon left home and went off to Camphill Special School in Pennsylvania. There he began a life quite different from what would have been possible for him at home, even with the best of special education classes in the state school system. Living in a house among a number of houses around the village, with other villagers, with house parents, children and farm animals, he entered a world that slowly began to work with him to evoke that special Camphill magic: to help him find all that he could express, manifest, develop.

My visits to Camphill School left a deep impression on me. There was a quality of life there that was different, brought to me through this younger, "retarded", "disabled" brother. After all, Jon had, from an early age, been teaching me something vital about observing the world around me, and myself, and what might be possible for us humans in it.

Jon was living in Camphill School, first with Erika, then with Adola. Our family visited on Saturdays. I was in California, going to college.

Jon lived in a house at school with his best friend, Alan, whose father and Harry would take turns driving the two kids home and back again for holidays and vacations. Jon and Alan couldn't have been more unlike one another. Jon was compulsively disorderly, and Alan

Music therapy.

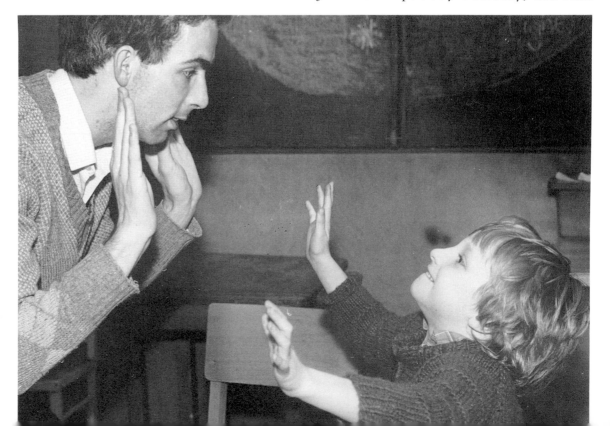

compulsively orderly. My mother tells a story: On a visit one Saturday to the school when Jon was about eight or nine, she said to Adola, "It must be hard for you having both boys in the house." Adola replied: "Well, we strive to have a balance." Almost as if to demonstrate, the two boys began to play together. In the schoolroom all the toys were kept in cupboards built around the periphery of the room, at floor level. Jon went in a circle around the edge of the room taking out every toy in the cupboard in front of him and depositing it on the floor in the middle of the room. Alan came along right behind him, putting each toy away exactly where it had been. This circumambulation continued without end, until it was time to stop. Balance. Harmony.

A vision of Camphill lodged deep within me: Standing on a hill in Beaver Run watching a new house being built. When Jon went to Beaver Run there were only three houses built. More were built "right under him". And this: Watching kites being flown in the breezes of a Pennsylvania spring. These physically "unable" children running in the wind, holding the strings and flying their kites high in the sky. And watching Jon grow to be a young man, ready to take his place in a society that was ready for him, in a Camphill village. And watching many "retarded", "disabled" and "non-functional" children work, study, grow and function. This image, this balanced relationship to others, and to the possibilities inside each of us, rooted itself deeply within me.

Jon grew up. He went from Beaver Run to Camphill Village, Copake, New York, with a couple of detours in between. I moved back from California to New York. My parents had aged. I had aged, also. I married. Had a family and home of my own. The convictions of my youth had faded somewhat. I had made my peace with the urban jungle, and had almost forgotten the vision of Camphill Special School as an island of sanity in a maddening world. Every now and then, though, the image of Camphill would return to me. There were visits to Jon and from him. I would contemplate the future, the purpose of that future. Sometimes I would regret the loss of the hopeful fantasies that had held me during my youth. But Jon, my parents, the entirety of that relationship didn't let that die altogether. Harry was deeply involved in the life of the village and devoted to Camphill. For him it had answered, albeit indirectly, a crying need that I am not sure he was ever aware of.

The question of maintaining Jon, and the Camphill villages, as time went on became more and more important to both the villages and the villagers, as well as to the families. Copake needed to start something, or something needed to be started, in any event, to prepare for the next period of time. And Carlo Pietzner, who, some twenty-five years before, had reached out to my brother, reached out to me and others. Carlo's far-reaching vision indicated that the villages, the community, needed to reach out and grow new shoots, sink new roots, or it would begin to stagnate. Something needed to be done to expand the community, to bring in those of us who were too "fortunate" to have had, by necessity, to go to Camphill. Those of us who now needed to recognize our connection with the choice of destiny that our siblings had made. And we had to recognize that their destinies also connected with ours. We needed to learn to be sensitive to this stream in which we were being carried.

One Family Day at Copake, in the fall of 1983, a group of brothers and sisters of the villagers gathered to discuss the need to continue this impulse. Gathered around the library, ranging in age from late teens to late fifties, married or single, with families or without, confused or sure of ourselves, we recognized that there was more destiny at work here than we had known. Brothers and Sisters of Camphill Village USA started to take shape.

Harry grew quite ill. He was clearly able to do less and less to support Jon or the village. His death was approaching, and by now he knew that. His last sickness, the slow approach of his end, was something in which we all, the entire Camphill family, participated. The village and all about it helped to prepare Jon for his father's death, and to connect us all.

Harry was near death. Jon needed me. And equally I needed him in the way I had come to understand I needed him when he was an infant, and he was my teacher about human reactions. I needed him to guide my spirit as it made yet another slow revolution around the ground beneath it in its search for some meaning to life on earth. I needed him to help me to recognize Camphill. Yes, he needed me too. To continue the relationship between him and family outside the village. To continue to be able to do the fun things with him that come from a visit home, a day out, planning for a Family Day. We needed each other.

Harry had struggled to go to Family Day, in October, 1986. It was difficult for him; he was very ill and surgery was scheduled for ten days later. It was the last thing which he did under his own power. The year before we had organized a discussion on death and dying as the principal activity of Family Day, and Harry had listened carefully as the questions concerning preparing for death had unfolded. He was changed by that day, I am sure of it. At that moment, I think, he realized that he had only a short time with which to prepare, a short while in which to develop whatever would be needed for the next step in his journey.

The village supported him. Through Jon, and through many others. People wrote to him; Kate Meinike sent him a card made of fallen leaves which hung over his bed for the last two months of his life. When he died, Jon and David Tarshus, Sylvia Bausman and Andy König were there, at the house, within three hours. Jon sat by his father and explored his wonderment at where he had gone.

Jon was not just Jon, he was a link to Camphill. And Camphill was not just where Jon lived, it was a link to a search that was my search also. Maybe all who are "Camphill" don't live in a village. Why did I feel, whenever I approached Copake, or Beaver Run, or Kimberton, that I was going home?

The Brothers and Sisters organization grew. It is quite strong now, each year doing more and more to contribute to the life of the village. There are studies of the anthroposophic basis of Camphill village life on Brothers and Sisters Day. There is the annual dinner dance. There is the growing community which will give birth to brother and sister organizations in other villages, which will someday help to encourage other young people to visit Camphill and possibly to make their lives, or a part of them, there.

There is the deepening bond which continues to grow between the village and us. It is like a tube through which flows communication, love, meaning, intention, destiny, hope. It is something which gives meaning to life on both sides of the connection, and allows activities in both places to be seen in the light of the realities of the other.

Camphill grows more central, day by day, to my image of the life of modern man and what is needed for it to continue. I am a proud server on the Board of Directors of Camphill Village USA, and on the board of trustees of the Camphill Association of North America. There is emerging, soon I hope, a truly American Camphill which will attract a new generation of American young people. And, as I watch Camphill places grow around the world, I wonder how many other times will the birth of some soul like Jonathan lead to such a family journey? There must be Camphill places to allow these stories to unfold. It is an obligation we all share: To continue to allow these special people to weave the webs of destiny with us, around us. Ask Jon. He knows.

Bill Prensky is a businessman in New York City.

What Camphill means to us

I speak several languages, studied at a prestigious US university, and had a management position in one of the world's top marketing companies. My wife was working too. We were on the fast track and a handicapped child did not fit into our world. But Karl John came into our lives, and he was handicapped. A convulsion and lack of oxygen right after birth caused brain

Wedding celebrations at Botton.

damage and mental retardation. Hyperactivity and other behavioural disturbances were the consequence. As he grew up, his retardation became more and more obvious. Coming home after a day's work or from a tiring business trip, he sometimes got on my nerves. When we went to a restaurant or on a weekend outing there was invariably some kind of upsetting scene so that it would have been better if we had stayed at home.

By chance we got to know John Byrde from the Camphill village Perceval, in St Prex, Switzerland, with whom we shared our worries. "If you move to Germany," he said, "see Hans Müller-Wiedemann." We did, and Karl John was accepted at the Camphill village Brachenreuthe on Lake Constance.

We were terribly upset about giving our son away. Yet we could hardly handle him any more (which must have been also due to my own immaturity). I was worried whether or not Karl John would be happy at Brachenreuthe. I was worried about him disrupting the peace in his house and in the village. I was worried about the co-workers well-being and whether they would keep Karl John. After all, I knew our hyperactive son!

Having Karl John sit still in a chair for five minutes was utterly amazing to us. And all this without tranquillizers as Dr Müller-Wiedemann predicted? Ha! We expected a phone call any day, saying: "Look, we tried everything, your son is just too difficult." And when we asked how difficult he was compared to the other handicapped children (that interested us at the time), the co-workers simply said that they loved him very much.

Well, Karl John could stay. He made enormous progress and became much more balanced. Since then, twelve years have elapsed and he is now living happily in the Camphill village for adults, Hermannsberg, also on Lake Constance. We are delighted. What happened? How was all the progress possible? We wanted to know more. Previously, a famous doctor told us that tranquillizers were the right thing for our son and there would be no harm or side effects.

My wife and I love our handicapped son and we are always happy when he comes home on vacation. But for more than ten years now the pattern has been more or less the same: After a few weeks we are worn out and, I am afraid to admit, glad Karl John can go back to

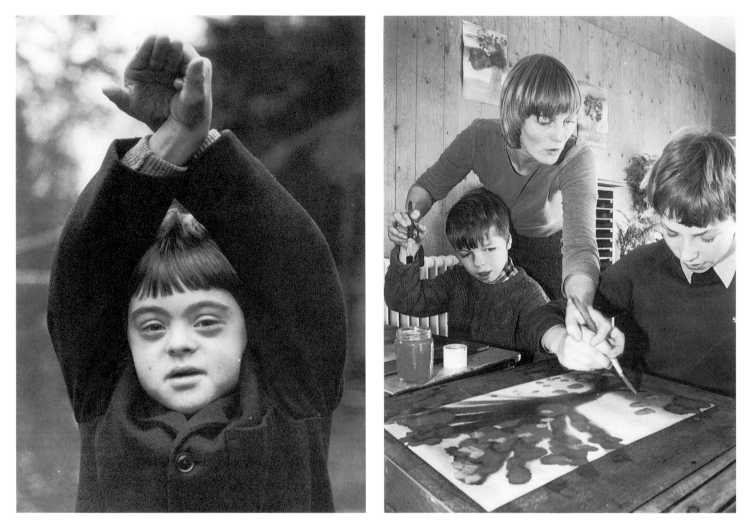

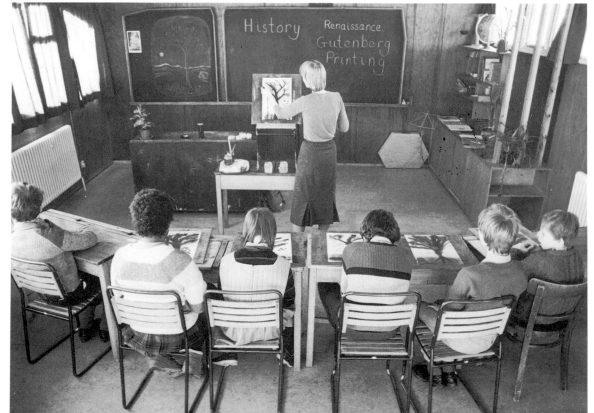

Painting lesson.

Camphill where we know there is a lot of trust, love and experience. We know that he is more balanced and more quiet at Camphill than at home. At Camphill, the co-workers usually live with up to ten handicapped in one house, thirty-five to forty-eight weeks a year! Where do they get their strength? And on top of it, when we visit them they welcome us, offer cake and coffee and radiate inner peace and warmth. Driving back home from a Camphill village on Lake Constance through the winding roads, the apple orchards and the forests of southern Germany, we always feel a unique sense of joy. Exactly the same feeling strikes us when we visit other Camphill places.

Gatherings, festivals, lectures and conferences with Camphillers and other parents with handicapped children, of which some have become close friends of ours, opened new doors for us. Anthroposophy was not new to us, but because of our many moves, we never gained depth. We wanted to know more and are now involved with Camphill and Anthroposophy. It has given us answers, changed our lives and values and given us deeper roots so that we could better master the problems of today's life; of which we have had our share!

Now, the ticks of my son and the other handicapped people no longer disturb me. Somehow they tend to have a positive effect. When I participate in a Bible evening, look into the villagers' eyes and listen to their simple and pure comments, it dawns on me what Camphill is all about. Thank you, Karl John for opening our eyes.

Alfred S. Heinrich is a businessman in Meggen, Switzerland.

The rings of fellowship

The occasion was the third Parents' Conference, the venue, the Grange Hall. Ninety parents were happily exchanging experiences and problems.

"He is so much better and loves his work."

"But they don't let him have his television, which he enjoys so much."

"He loved his Granny very much, we could not possibly have taken him to the funeral, he would have been so upset."

"What a blessing, with scanning and abortion there will be so much less handicap around."

"But they don't believe in abortion."

Discussions like this, which raised questions which could only be touched on in a conference, led to the forming of the first Ring in Droitwich in March 1983. A group of about twenty-four, four from within Camphill, met three times a year. They strongly believed that there was a deep-felt need for those "within Camphill" and for those who lived on the "fringe", to develop greater understanding of each others points of view.

It was realized that there were many parents and friends who only partially understood the anthroposophical approach to life, and those who were already following the principles of Anthroposophy were glad to be able to discuss important issues with those who might hold different points of view.

The subjects discussed have been wide-ranging. For instance, medical ethics and the unborn child; the temperaments; life after death; the threefold social order; relationships, and others.

It has been a great experience to spend three days in a year discussing matters of consuming interest with people who have come together with the bond of knowing a handicapped person, or being interested in Anthroposophy. I am sure those who are part of the other Rings feel equally stimulated and rewarded in their discussions.

Jean Davidson

"Mornin' everybody"

Sports day

Well, ain't the birds chirpin' and the frogs burpin' this mornin'? Somebody around here must have been livin' right, else we couldn't 'a got that nice little bit of rain yesterday. We sure could use some more, but you got to be thankful for what you get.

Say, speakin' of what you get, Steve told me about a note that some or'nary house mother dropped into his box, the one who couldn't do her dishwash, with all sorts of remarks on it listed in categories with numbers. Steve said she must be tryin' to show him she knows how to count.

Well, she seemed to be sort of mixed, happy-sad, because she said that when she finally got her water back, the hot came on faster, and she didn't have to waste a truckload of water just waitin' for it, and why, after all these months of askin' Steve to do something about it, did the situation suddenly get better, when Steve could have raised the pressure long ago and fixed everything.

Steve was stumped. He asked me how you go about explainin', or even tryin' to bother to inform someone like that, about how the pipes in the basement of her house are a tad bigger and a smidge longer than most, and how they get full of hot water when someone is using it, and then all that water sits there when they're not usin' it and cools off. And the real reason it comes on faster is not because of the pressure, but because Tom Sholl (bless his heart and our pocketbook) spent a good part of last week riggin' up a system Steve designed to *keep* hot water in those big pipes, whether someone was usin' them or not?

She even had the gall to poke at Steve's childhood and say how awful it must have been. Steve told me he had a wonderful childhood. He says he even had a dumptruck just like me, he used to play with in the neighbour's sand box, only it was red instead of green, and that warmed my heart. Then he went on to say I was the only woman he ever wanted to marry 'cause I always did what he told me to do, and didn't never give him no back talk. Then I almost turned as red as that dumptruck Steve had when he was a kid.

Well, I shouldn't be botherin' you with all this, 'cause the real reason I wanted to get into your mornin' mail was because Steve was sittin' there watchin' that rain yesterday when the detective inside of him started scratchin'. Next thing you know, off he goes to see if all those dag-blasted hoses wuz turned off. Now over in the field vegetable patch folks got their act together and everything was fine. But back by Mornin' Star garden, in spite of the fact that there's two houses just a sittin' there starin' out, the hose cocks wuz still on after we'd had a good half-hour of rain. Now that means Old Red was puttin' in extra time. His time in electricity is close to 3000 watts per hour, which comes to about 33 cents, and that's not a crime, but if you take into account that his days are numbered and the $2000 plus it's going to cost to replace him, it gets a little more stiff. And pumps is famous for going under on a holiday or a weekend when everything costs more, if you can get it at all.

So if you garden folk would work out some kind of deal with the Sycamore Linden folks for if and when it does rain, things'll be better.

"Sophie", USA. Sophie is the name of Steve Chamberlin's dumptruck. A series of articles appeared in the weekly news-sheet of the Kimberton Hills village under this name.

Excerpt from a diary

I am at Camphill Farm and have come for a two-week trial visit. This afternoon I played frisbee with Geoffrey, Anette and a friend. After a good session of fun we got ready for supper, which is very light.

In Labora House there are five of us, and our house-master is Lawrence Adler. The five of us are all boys: Jeff, Gary, Richard, myself and Hamish. After supper Gary and I did the dishes. Then at 7:45 there was an assembly for the forty villagers and staff. Gary is the chairman of the Village Assembly, so he did the address. It was very interesting. There were points on gardening, punctuality, films etc. They also welcomed me to the farm, which I thought was quite something.

Eventually the meeting ended on a good musical note — we sang. Back at Labora House, Gary, Jeff and I had coffee then went and chatted upstairs for a while before turning in for the night.

Monday, April 27: My first day on the farm. At breakfast this morning we all said Happy

Hermanus Camphill School, South Africa.

Birthday to Hamish. Now it is time for action. I start with the farmers. I meet Tim and the others. There is Charles, Mark, Alan and Grant. Charles and I went to herd the cattle into the pastures. Then I helped Grant clean the cow's kraal . . . back to work at 2:30.

Jeff is plucking chickens with Tim and Allen. I went with Charles to fetch the cow herd back to the camp, then we went to get the chickens from the shed to get ready for slaughter. Then we went to the dairy and I took an interest in the milking. The day's work was over at 5:00. Hamish wanted a dance at Labora (for his birthday). A lot of villagers turned up. It was a good dance.

Tuesday, April 28: We went to the goats' paddock and picked up all the dead trees and branches so Tim could burn them in a trench. After work Gary, Jeff and I played table tennis. We were joined for a while by Lawrence. It was good fun.

Wednesday, April 29: Charles, Grant and I helped Tim sow the seeds from the tractor by hand. Then I helped Anne clean the floor of the dairy. Having finished it was time for lunch at 12:00. It was a good lunch cooked by Barbara. Tonight is shop night.

Thursday, April 30: We went to the barn where we milled the grain. Back at Labora we had supper with a visitor, Gary's girlfriend Barbara.

Friday, May 1: This will be my fifth day here in the new month of May. Charles and I went and chucked rocks aside while Tim was mowing the grass. Then Mark and I joined Anne in the dairy helping her with the cheese and milking the cows. After supper there was a social evening for everyone. It was a pleasant evening, with dancing.

Monday, May 4: The vet came to test the cows for pregnancy. There were today at least three cows pregnant of five that he checked. The evening meal was fine with tea done by Gary. After supper we played bingo. It was fun — no gambling though!

Tuesday, May 5: I went to the dairy and helped Anne make butter. I did the churning while she prepared the bowls, and so on. While we were making the butter we sang some songs. I

94

was invited to the Old Farm House for lunch, it was very pleasant. In the afternoon there were groups. I was in two: from 2:24 to 3:45 I was doing folk dancing, then 4:00 to 5:00 I did music. It was fun, especially the music.

Wednesday, May 6: I went to the dairy to help Anne make yoghurt. Anne steamed the milk in a pot in which I checked the heat with a thermometer. After that we poured the liquid into jars and let it set.

Thursday, May 7: Today it is field day around the houses. Everyone works outside around the gardens. We started digging a trench and filling it with rubble. While Jeff was breaking the rubble I was digging and shifting the sand.

Friday, May 8: My final working day on the farm. This afternoon at 3:00 a bus is coming to collect us to go to Cape Town. We are going to watch some play at a Waldorf School. They will be Greek plays, but in English.

The trip was nice — going through places like Houhoek, Strand and Somerset West. We arrived in time. The first play was about Helen of Troy. It was good. After that there was an interval. Then the final play was a comedy. It was hilarious. After that we started back to Hermanus. We arrived back at 12:40 am. What an evening it was!

Saturday, May 9: The morning's work is picking up rubble for the trench. So off we went in the truck and loaded up with rubble. Then we came back and started working on the trench. Two young kids from Castor, Stephen and Raymond, came and helped us. Eventually I had to stop, as I was invited to lunch at Melissa's house. Ulrike and Tim are the house parents there. It was Tim I worked for and the reason for the invitation was to say thank you for the work. After a good lunch I said good-bye to my farm friends. In the afternoon Stephen and Raymond played with Jeff, Enorietha and myself. We played frisbee and football.

Evening came, so to the Bible study. I read a passage and put the candle out. The meal was fine for all of us.

Sunday, May 10: My last day here at Camphill. The two weeks have been pleasant and very interesting for me. The morning started at the chapel with a service; then we had breakfast. Now I am packing my bags. In Labora everyone is upset that I am leaving. They are threatening to tie me up to keep me from going, but they know that one day I might come back.

Thank you Labora. It has been pleasant being among true and good people. See you sometime. Here I end my report.

Peter Johnson, South Africa.

A village portrait — Fred Malamed

I did not believe at first
that you would walk out of a painting,
without first pausing
to change your clothes
and remove the other traces;
but then I began to recognize
that there had always been
a special quality in your walk,
the hidden genius of a Chaplin
confined to canvas and paint
and constant scrutiny, the self-

awareness and distinct melancholy
of a body fashioned by a brush —
with death.

I saw you long ago
returning from a sun-spent day;
your easel under your arm,
your hat slightly shrunken
and with a giddy tilt,
your shadow drunken on the ground,
a victim of sun and paint.

I saw you as you saw yourself
and as I see you now
when the sun returns, and you,
you amble past a row of sunflowers
without even turning your head,
and yet you always turn to me
as soon as I enter
into painting distance,
your greeting, sunlike, open,
brushing away at shadows . . .

but now it is my turn
to paint — your yellow slicker,
worn in the manner of Provence
and only a hundred years out of style;
a bunch of parsley, held
like a bouquet — with both hands —
in place of the cluster of brushes;
and the scrunched straw hat,
put on with both hands too;
and yet I have lost your gait,
it seems to have wandered
far from my canvas, your left leg
lifting, as if freeing itself
from some subtle entanglement.

Andrew Hoy, formerly of Kimberton Hills, USA, has been a Camphill co-worker for many years.

Chapter 5

The extended circle –
a Camphill portrait

The Scottish region

Friedwart Bock

The life and work of Camphill began in Scotland on June 1, 1940, after about a year's activity at the simple manse at Kirkton. Since its birth the work of the movement has grown, spreading out into Europe and beyond. The work in Scotland remained centred on Deeside for thirty two years, with the growth into other areas only beginning in 1972. Today, with eight centres in the Scottish Highlands, two in the Lowlands and one in the Southern Uplands, Camphill in Scotland extends right across the country from the north-east to the south-west and maintains the full spectrum of therapeutic impulses that has been developed in the past half century. Two villages, two schools, four centres for young adults, two for adolescents and one for old people are now established here.

The Camphill Schools, Aberdeen

There are three Camphill schools on the Camphill, Murtle and Cairnlee estates to the north of the River Dee, a few miles from the city of Aberdeen.

Landscape at Kirkton House, near Aberdeen.

The estates are near the sea, and the sea fog, the haar, reaches inland bringing sea smells and a chilly reminder of the sea's proximity. At times the smells of the city's fishing industry come on the wind, but normally the air is clear, stirred by a bracing breeze. In summer, the experience of the light is dominant. Towards the west the purple hills and Grampian Highlands beckon and speak of ancient ages of the earth. The River Dee runs its rapid course from the Grampians to the sea. The Dee can be formidable when in flood, or when it carries huge chunks of ice during the spring thaw while the salmon struggle upstream towards the river's source.

Camphill is close to an ancient ford where the Knights Templars and Hospitallers crossed to their nearby preceptory. At Murtle the valley narrows, and the river follows a straight course towards the sea unimpeded by boulder banks or granite outcrops.

The three estates are self-contained and weaving the three together is an ongoing task. Communication is vital, and a fleet of vehicles takes care of the transport from one estate to the next. Murtle and Camphill, the two larger estates, have their own halls for assembly, games, cultural events and festival celebrations, so the need to travel is reduced; all the activities can take place on home ground.

The main task of Camphill Aberdeen is the work with school-age children and adolescents in need of special care. Curative education has been practised there for half a century, and the sixteen houses on the three properties provide homes for 170 children, adolescents, staff and their families.

The three streams in the work of Camphill — therapy, school and home life — seek to bring help and healing to the children. As man is a being of body, soul and spirit, so do these three realms answer the children's particular needs and are woven together in their day. In the course of a day, a child may have trampoline therapy for his spatial co-ordination, and then return to his class of ten-year-olds busy painting with their class teacher. The class may be having their first geography block and be painting a picture of mountains and a loch. When school draws to an end, and after some reading and writing practice, the child will go back to his house for lunch. If he is in a wheelchair, other children will help him up the steep path. There could be a birthday in the house, with cake, ice cream and other surprises to share.

Camphill's school, called St John's, began in 1947 as a small Waldorf school for the co-workers' children, and other children from the city. In 1951 Dr König opened the school to all the "children in need of special care". This soon proved to be beneficial and today seventeen classes are at work in the schoolhouses Pyrite, Mica, Tourmaline and Carnelian.

The teaching staff work intensively for three hours a week, and in weekend workshops, with the questions of how the educational ideas of Rudolf Steiner can be more fully applied to different age groups and individual children, and how teachers can improve their skills for the work. The therapists also come together to undertake research and develop individual therapies, including speech, colour, light, art, play, music and physiotherapy.

Home life and child guidance are the task of the houseparents group. In their meetings, problems of individual children, or groupings of children can be led towards resolution by efforts to gain insight, and by developing new approaches. The houseparents form the core of the house communities, and also tutor the students studying curative education.

Camphill is connected to the wider community through three parents' groups, the Friends of Camphill, two consultants, and external members of the council. Within Camphill there are diverse regional and inter-regional groups which provide links with the wider Camphill movement.

The geographical centre is Camphill Hall. Standing at the side of Murtle House, its domed roof overlooks the valley of the Dee. As well as being an assembly hall for the schools, it is used by the whole Camphill movement for regular conferences and seminars. The hall was built with the help of the whole movement, and opened in September 1962, the year that marked the sixtieth birthday of its founder, Dr König.

From the early history of Newton Dee*

St John's fire, Midsummer at Murtle House, Aberdeen.

In the course of 1944, a group of about twelve young lads had been admitted to Camphill who presented different challenges to us from the more handicapped children. They had, for the most part, been before the courts, and in the terms of the day were categorized as mildly, or less mildly, delinquent.

Although Thomas Weihs ran a tiny school farm on the Camphill estate for the benefit of these lads, the problem they presented to us, and to the other children, were at times formidable. But what to do?

One day we were struck by a notice in the *Aberdeen Press and Journal* to the effect that an estate of 173 acres, more or less adjoining Murtle, was up for sale, as the owner of the estate had died. This was a Mrs Johnson, a renowned Edwardian beauty on Deeside, who had been widowed early. For many years, Mrs Johnson lived in a world of her own, together with the memories of her late husband, surrounded by a few devoted servants (one of whom we knew) until she was no longer able to look after herself and was admitted to a private nursing home in nearby Banchory.

I mention all this because in the first months at Newton Dee, her gentle yet withdrawn spirit was quite tangible to the extent that she was an element of "poltergeist" in the main house, but in no way frightening or offensive. We had the impression that the presence of the children was welcome and helpful.

Negotiations with Mrs Johnson's executors began, but the situation looked fairly hopeless because the war was just over and we had no money at all. W.F. Macmillan, who had procured Camphill estate or us, suggested that his sister Helen, Alistair Macmillan's aunt, buy the new estate, which she did for the sum of £11,000. As with the Camphill estate, we subsequently repaid the money for Newton Dee to the Macmillan family.

* This section is by Anke Weihs

View over the Dee River from Murtle House, and Camphill Hall, Murtle, Aberdeen.

We moved into Newton Dee house during Advent 1945 with our twelve delinquent lads. Thomas Weihs, Eileen Slaughter, Reg and Molly Bould, and myself to begin with. There was something very dark about Newton Dee estate owing to the density of its large conifers, a big proportion of which fell later in the freak storm of January 1953. However, the house too was dark — chocolate-brown corridors, very dark wood panelling, and very few saving graces. In addition we had to buy ex-army iron beds and other furniture, and the lifestyle of the delinquents, who soon increased in number, did little to relieve the spartan aspects of life in early Newton Dee.

Yet, there was one outstanding lovely feature when we took over: the flowers. Broad bands of blue scilla lined the whole drive, which was then dirt, right up to the main road. The garden produced familiar and unfamiliar flowers in such profusion from spring onward that we filled four large laundry baskets every weekend with flowers for Camphill, Heathcot, Murtle, and The Christian Community in town. In addition, there were all kinds of exotic flowering shrubs and bushes throughout the estate. Owing to the activities of our lads, but also of some of our horticulturally ambitious staff, this touching paradise soon vanished.

Life in the first year at Newton Dee was hard, rudimentary, and fairly restricted. The farm belonging to the estate was only to become vacant at Martinmas 1946. The entire estate was neglected and run down, and before the farm was taken over, fences had to be renewed everywhere and incessant repair work carried out. But life was never at a standstill. The exploits of our boys on the estate and outside brought the police almost daily to our door, and the respectability of Bieldside, the local town, took years to recover from this truly spicy period.

At Martinmas 1946, the old one-legged farmer, McBain, moved away and we took full possession of the farm and farmhouse, both very run down, and daunting in their lack of appeal. Thomas, city bred and a student of medicine, read up on farming and with his characteristic power of application, he, together with the boys, six ponies and a sizable herd of cows, began to farm. It was truly a Homeric time! Indeed, our boys were convinced that he was the reincarnated Odysseus. Butter was churned daily for the different estates, and large numbers of hens, ducks and geese were kept.

Yet there was another aspect of Newton Dee that few are perhaps aware of. As the approved school system made considerable progress after the war, our "delinquents" were gradually adequately placed elsewhere. We then took a group of adults with psychiatric problems after having studied Steiner's lectures on pastoral medicine. The group was carried by Peter Roth as priest and Thomas as doctor-farmer. We set aside Newton Dee cottage and the farmhouse for what, in hindsight, we may call the first village seedling. This pastoral-medical attempt dissolved, giving way to the gradual development of craft training for handicapped boys.

The actual village impulse surfaced only in 1954–55 with the move to Botton, but the initial vision was born at Newton Dee.

Newton Dee Village Community

Newton Dee Village Community could once have been described as completely rural, but with the city of Aberdeen spreading in all directions, the village now has something of an urban character. Becoming a village had both outer and inner implications, and throughout we set ourselves the aim of proving that so-called handicapped adults can work, just as the Schools set out to prove that handicapped children can be educated. The content of the village lectures, given by Dr König during 1962–64, were a necessary guide, and have remained our inspiration.* They showed us that living and working together in mutual benefit would build up the "village attitude", enabling the co-workers and handicapped people to form a real community as part of the locality, and not cut off from it.

Our status as a Department of Employment sheltered workshop is important to us, lending emphasis to employment. From the beginning, our aim within the craft production area was to make good quality articles for sale on the open market. Our workshops are involved in toy-making, textile weaving, woodwork, doll-making, tie dying, basket making, and metal work. Markets were gradually found all over the country, and a level of productivity together with a consistently high quality has to be maintained. Another area of constant work is the land, which gives employment to farmers, gardeners and estate workers. The farm with its Ayrshire cows provides milk and yoghurt for the village and the Camphill Schools. We grow most of our own vegetables, and also care for the estate.

A store was built, and has since expanded, which supplies a wide range of groceries, household goods and health foods. The store is open to the public and provides the needs of other Camphill centres in the local area.

In 1971 a hall was built overlooking the village green. Phoenix Hall, designed by Gabor Tallo, has a stage and auditorium seating 250 people, and also a retail shop, office and coffee bar, making it into a real social centre for the village and the local area, as well as a worthy home for our cultural and social endeavours.

Over the years we have been slowly integrated into our locality. We decided very early on that we wanted to be an ordinary village, so we took down the signs which said private, enabling our food store, bakery, laundry, coffee bar and retail shop to have a growing outside market. Local people wander through the village and use its public facilities.

There is an active architects office within Newton Dee, which designs buildings for Britain and overseas. Its origins go back to the arrival in 1949 of architect Paul Bay. Some of the Newton Dee co-workers also helped to establish the Aberdeen Waldorf School. Newton Dee also offers an introductory course in Anthroposophy and village life which our younger co-workers, many from overseas, can attend.

In 1988 there were 185 people living in eighteen houses of various sizes, including a "group home", on the estate. The newest addition, Francis House, has facilities for extra care and therapy space for ageing and frail residents, and those who need special rhythms in their daily life.

* *In Need of Special Understanding*, Camphill Press, Botton 1986.

Living together, with its simple but strong attitude of caring for each other, was very attractive, and still today at Newton Dee the emphasis is placed on the quality of the life that is lived together.

Newton Dee started with sixty people, of whom about forty were later registered as disabled. By 1970, the estate had almost doubled its population, and was being asked by doctors, parents, and later by the Social Services Department to take on those classified as "mentally ill". Today, Newton Dee is ideally placed to play a part in the Community Care programme which is developing in Britain. Those people who were once taken out of society, into hospitals often in remote areas, are now being brought back into the towns. Often employment is not available, and society is generally not ready or willing to help. Placed as it is in a peaceful rural landscape, but with the city at its door, and with a strong commitment to working and living together, Newton Dee expects to play an active part in the future.

Ochil Tower School

In the past thirty years, an international movement has grown from small beginnings on the lower Deeside. In January 1972, the first Scottish development outside Aberdeen was established. Ochil Towers, a six-acre property in Perthshire, was bought. It is the only Camphill school in Scotland outside Aberdeen and lies in the royal burgh of Auchterarder, overlooking the Ochil Hills. The first nine children at the school moved there from Aberdeen, and they were soon joined by nine others.

The outer development of this school reflects an inner development of community building and ongoing curative education, together with many cultural and social pursuits. Ochil Tower provides a central venue for Camphill's Neighbourhood meetings, as well as for concerts, eurythmy performances, retreats and small conferences.

Templehill

Less than a year after Ochil Tower started, Templehill was purchased with the help of a gift, and established by the Camphill Schools, Aberdeen. This was the initiative of the late Thomas and Anke Weihs. It lies twenty-five miles from Aberdeen near Auchenblae and consists of a large house and eight and a half acres of land, including a large garden.

For the first seven years, Templehill was home to a group of people with widely differing disabilities, ranging in age from young children to adults. All of them needed an environment in which to achieve and express maturity and dignity by taking on responsibility for others in a free and creative community. The designation for this community was aptly "a community for mutual help."

In 1979 the direction changed. A second house was opened and Templehill became a centre for further education and social therapy for adolescents and young adults with special needs with a renewed emphasis on working together. In the following year a small seventeen-acre adjoining farm was added, which extended the range and variety of the work and involvement of the students. By the very nature of its remoteness and the severe degree of handicap of its students, Templehill is only now gradually becoming integrated with the locals.

Blair Drummond

The driving force that lived in Anke Weihs took her to many locations in Scotland in search of other suitable places. In 1975 she found a spectacular Victorian building near Stirling: Blair Drummond House. With its mighty, square tower and some eighty rooms, it stands together

Blair Drummond, Stirling, Scotland.

with some out-buildings in seventeen acres of parkland overlooking Scotland's Safari Park. The house came on the market for a very reasonable figure. The purchase was made with the help of bank loans and loans from other Camphill centres. The co-workers were able to completely repay the loans by 1985.

In January 1976, the first co-workers and a few trainees moved in, and with incredible energy and ingenuity set to work on major internal structural changes. The first, third and fourth floors became self-contained units; and the second, with its public rooms and long passage ways, provided a workshop, classroom, large common room and chapel. In the following ten years another unit was established in the east wing, and the clock-house converted into two more units. Gradually the out-buildings were transformed into workshops for woodwork, metal work, and weaving, and a bakery. Recently a garden centre and basket workshop were established.

Corbenic

Two years after the founding of Blair Drummond, Anke and Thomas Weihs found yet another place suitable for the Camphill impulse: Drumour Lodge, a former hotel for hunting parties. It lies in the Highland hills near Dunkeld in Perthshire, and was renamed Corbenic College. The tranquillity of the hills in which it lies, and the sound of the rushing waters of the River Braan running below, provide a wonderfully peaceful and refreshing setting.

*Corbenic College,
Dunkeld, Perthshire, a
former hunting lodge.
Opposite: Corbenic
College today.*

Corbenic's development was "uphill". There were years of struggle to upgrade the house, to find additional land and the means with which to cover the enormous costs, to meet the requirements of the fire regulations, and roof repairs. Around this need, the newly established Scottish Camphill Neighbourhood rallied together. Help was extended by Blair Drummond and Ochil Tower.

Beannachar

In the same year that Corbenic was purchased, Aberdeen expanded also. This time it was across the Dee, and not too far from the former Heathcot House. The large manor house, once part of the Banchory-Devenick estate, was renamed Beannachar. This is Gaelic for Banchory and is thought to mean "blessed community". The house, just outside the city boundary, is gracious and beautiful. It is built of the local grey, mica-speckled granite, but it needed a great deal of interior work to bring it up to the required building standards. It was purchased in 1978 to be a horticultural training centre for anyone who wished to work on the land. This not only included the handicapped students from the schools, but also those who had been in prison, or who were searching for more meaning to their lives.

Although land-based, Beannachar provides for a far wider range of needs. There is a walled vegetable and fruit garden and a smallholding with a few cows, pigs, sheep and poultry on fifteen acres of grassland. There is also a laundry and a herb garden with its own workshop where herb teas, ointments, tinctures and lotions are made.

104

Loch Arthur Village

During this period of rapid growth the Scottish Neighbourhood as a whole was aware that many training centres were being founded, yet Newton Dee was the only village community in Scotland. This meant that the waiting list was so long that there were no places available for those who had come to the end of their time in other Camphill centres. In 1983, a meeting was held to which parents and all those interested in a new village project, were invited. Thomas Weihs, already gravely ill, spoke full of enthusiasm, outlining a new concept for the inclusion of handicapped people into a village setting. This was to be his last public appearance, and the words he spoke left us with a challenge that we still strive to meet.

At the meeting the decision was taken to look for a suitable property. Finally, in the summer of 1984, a five-hundred-acre estate was purchased through the joint strength of the Camphill Village Trust. The property, the Lotus estate near Dumfries in south-west Scotland, included a main house, a garden cottage and various other buildings. Three young couples from Newton Dee village with a variety of professional skills, and one couple from England, all with their young families, formed the core group of the new village community, which was called Loch Arthur. Newton Dee also gave considerable financial and material help to enable farm stock and machinery to be purchased.

From the beginning, severely handicapped adults were admitted and they needed a great deal of both soul and physical care. It was a challenge to find simple yet meaningful work for them, as well as to run the farm and look after five hundred acres. Not only had the land to be looked after, but also the houses. Here, the daily cleaning and cooking provided a warm and light mode of essential work. One of the very physically handicapped young men became the founder of the creamery, and it became his task to churn the day's butter for everyone. The land needed clearing so wheelbarrowing was essential, as was help with the small flock of sheep. Not only hands to open and close gates, but bodies to block the sheep as they were moved from field to barn, or run along the paths were needed. There were those who learnt to milk by hand, and others helped by carrying feed. In the garden there was composting and vegetable harvesting, and for those who could not manage work on the land, a wool shop was started, where teasing was an essential yet simple task.

Now the pioneering years have passed and Loch Arthur is well accepted and respected by the local community and looks to the future with strength and hope.

Simeon Care for the elderly

As Camphill became older, so to did its co-workers. Each time a new children's unit was built a small flat was included, so that those who were not so young any more could still live with the children, but no longer in the centre of activity. But even this is only manageable while people are still able to look after themselves. In 1980, forty years after its beginnings, two ladies, already in their eighties, needed more care than we could adequately provide. It became clear that in the school setting with its busy timetable, the slow and quiet lifestyle required at this age could not be catered for. Not only our staff, but friends who had supported us from the beginning were also looking for a place where one's whole destiny was recognized, and not just the physical body cared for.

In 1984, after lengthy discussions with members from the schools, villages and local authorities, one of the small one-storeyed houses was rented from the Camphill Schools, and Simeon Care for the Elderly was set up as a separate charitable company. Caranoc, together with its twin house Whithorn, was originally built as a children's unit. Cairnlee estate, on which it is built, is small and quiet. The first ten residents included ladies from Aberdeen, a villager from Newton Dee, a retired Christian Community priest from England and parents of Camphill co-workers.

View over Loch Arthur, Dumfries.

One challenge was how to live a Camphill community life, which is strongly anthroposophical and Christian Community oriented, in harmony with those who came from traditional Aberdeen homes. Another was to make each individual feel truly at home. Yet another challenge was to convince the authorities of our feasibility. On the one hand we were "private", yet in contrast to the normal private homes, we were not out to make money. Community living allowed us to have a much lower ratio of staff to residents because we did not work in shifts as is normal in such establishments, nor did we receive wages. Simeon's name was soon proclaimed in the right quarters, and many requests now come from social workers and hospital staff. The local Health Centre is particularly impressed with Simeon for, although it is not registered as a nursing home, it provides care for its residents right through to their death.

In 1987 Camphill Schools vacated the adjoining house, Whithorn, and after the necessary alterations it was possible to admit another six residents. The two houses give many possibilities for interchange, visiting, or coming together for bigger events. The surroundings, with lawns, gardens, local walks and shops and bus stop near by, and the versatility of the small St Martin's hall within the grounds, make a wonderful setting for the elderly. There is a croquet club at Simeon, which also has members from Bieldside village.

It is the aim of Simeon to learn, together with the residents, to recognize the meaning of old age in our time, so as to make the last years of life harmonious and fruitful.

Tigh a' Chomainn

As the years passed by, our ideas began to change. In the beginning it was felt that some segregation was necessary: the older maladjusted boys were separated from the older girls, and the blind children had a special unit to themselves. Gradually this changed as we discovered the mutual help that one type of child could give to another. Not only did we change, but so did the type and age range of the children who were sent to us.

Slowly, additional special schools were provided for the handicapped child. Thus we no longer received so many young children, but more teenagers. Then the government provided more opportunities for teenagers, and once again the age of the people coming to us rose. We had to introduce a seniors programme. In 1986 an opportunity arose to begin a new community to establish a half-way house outside the school setting, yet within the locality so there would be mutual support and interchange.

In 1987 Tigh a' Chomainn was set up. The name is Gaelic and means "House of the Community". A sturdy granite house, once the manse of the church next to it, was bought in the nearby village of Peterculter. The house stands in its own grounds and looks down to the River Dee and the rolling farmland beyond. It accommodates seven residents and three co-workers. Shops and buses are close by which gives the residents the opportunity to do their shopping conveniently, and to catch a bus to work.

Tigh a' Chomainn is registered with the Social Work Department for sixteen to forty-five-year-olds, and this relatively wide age range makes provision for the older person who still wishes to attempt greater independence. The length of stay is not fixed, and depends on the time taken to reach as much independence as possible.

The residents normally go out to work or follow a training or college course. They are encouraged to develop their independence in looking after themselves, seeing to their laundry and personal hygiene. They learn to cope with public transport, budget and look after their money. Katie works at a supermarket, John and Gary attend college, Adrian and Scott work as groundsmen at Murtle, and William is doing a plumber's apprenticeship at a local technical college.

*Mists over the Yorkshire
Moors in Botton Village.*

The English and Welsh region

Michael Luxford

The Sheiling Schools

Within a decade of establishing its home in Scotland the call came to Camphill and Dr König to establish curative education in England. But how and where? As almost inevitably happens, the call came from the children themselves. Dr König had become the medical consultant to a pioneering venture in Bristol, St Christopher's School for children in need of special care, founded by Miss Catherine Grace, OBE. With Dr König's gifts as a physician, the number of pupils seeking admission soon grew beyond the dimensions of the school, so it was proposed to open a hostel. This was easier said than done: Bristol had suffered severely in the wartime bombing and houses were at a premium.

However, towards the end of 1948 a large Georgian house came on the market in Thornbury, twelve miles from Bristol. Thornbury House, with its walled garden and six acres of fertile ground, seemed an opportunity not to be missed, and, after a hurried search for funds, the house was purchased. It opened its doors to pupils of St Christopher's in May 1949. At the same time, on the other side of Bristol, Wraxall House had been purchased to provide an additional hostel for St Christopher's. Both of these houses received substantial support from co-workers who came from Camphill at Aberdeen. Tilla König, Dr König's wife, was part of this group.

Camphill's move into England was not confined to the South-West: in the South there was similar activity. The grandparents of a child in the Camphill Schools were living in Ringwood in Hampshire, on the edge of the New Forest. In 1948 they asked Dr König if he could make use of their home, the Sheiling, a Scottish name for "a shelter". On seeing the house, Dr König expressed his delight, both in the house and the whole area. He remarked that here a children's village could develop, and he foresaw a place with many wooden houses. Dr König pointed to the aridity of the sandy soil surrounding the Sheiling, where little more than gorse and heather flourished. He spoke of the need for work on the soil: "Only when people have worked the land with love can there be a school." This pioneering work was undertaken with enthusiasm by young members from Camphill, who subsequently became the nucleus of the group that developed the Sheiling School at Ringwood.

The early involvement of these young people, who already had experience in curative education in Scotland, led to the seeds for Camphill's work in England being planted both in the South-West at Thornbury, and in the South at Ringwood. These two schools jointly became the Sheiling Curative Schools in 1951. The opening of the Sheiling Schools, as the first venture independent of the Camphill Schools in Aberdeen, marked the beginning of the Camphill movement.

In 1952 another house in Thornbury was acquired, Thornbury Park, a spacious residence with a walled garden standing amid beautiful trees in parkland. Thornbury House and Wraxhall were sold and Camphill took on its own identity in the grounds of Thornbury Park. In 1953 a house for the use of the older boys was bought. This was the Hatch, which had been the town's grammar school in the mid seventeenth century.

Over the years, considerable progress has been made at Thornbury and Ringwood. The school in Thornbury began its work with spastic children as the peacefulness of Thornbury

Above: Thornbury Park House, Bristol. Midsummer fun (above right), Parsifal play (below), and York mystery cycle performance (opposite), Botton Village, Yorkshire.

Park seemed most suitable for these children who need a slow pace of life with specific therapies and nursing care in addition to their educational needs. This work was carried on until 1963 when autistic children were also admitted. Houses, classrooms, therapy rooms, a hall, and farm steadings have been built. The existence in earlier centuries of places of healing in this part of the Severn Valley has found a new expression.

The verdant and fertile surroundings Thornbury contrast strongly with the sandy grounds of the Sheiling Community in Ringwood. But while it has been difficult to create productive soil out of the sand of the New Forest, the Ringwood Community has been fertile ground for the development of social and therapeutic impulses in the 1970s and 80s. Following on from

110

what it has been offering as schooling for the younger child, there is now a college for school-leavers and a training course for those over nineteen years old. The latter is strongly orientated towards the land, and the nearby Sturts Farm was acquired to create an independent venture providing agricultural work for these young adults.

Folly Farm, adjacent to the school, also provides for those who have left Ringwood College, and, together with Sturts Farm, comprises the Sheiling Farm group. Nearby is Folly Farm Waldorf School, a school for the normally developing child based on the educational principles of Rudolf Steiner, and in recent years close links have been formed with the Ringwood Community. Since 1978 Ringwood has also hosted the first two years of the Ringwood-Botton Eurythmy School training, the third and fourth years being held at Botton Village in Yorkshire. After all these years Dr König's remark about the Sheiling becoming a children's village has been realized, and there are also quite a few wooden houses!

Botton Village

Fourteen years after work with children had begun in Aberdeen, a parent put a crucial question to Dr König: "What is to happen when our sons and daughters are no longer children, but become adults?" It had become apparent to the parents of these first children that despite all opinions to the contrary the belief that they held in the developmental possibilities of their "retarded children" had been justified. But how were these youngsters to find a place in the adult world which would include work and social integration? From Dr König the parents acquired the conviction that despite daunting odds the "handicapped child" can, with love, guidance and appropriate education, grow into adult life able to make a valuable and worthy contribution to society and the world.

He had a vision of the communities which would be needed for the handicapped adults and their helpers. There would have to be work on the land, in the houses and the craft workshops producing articles for sale. A cultural life would have to be fostered, as in the Camphill schools, but with the difference that this would not be created for the handicapped, but with them. Interdependence would have to grow between the helper and the helped, and out of this mutuality a new and more appropriate social life would be established. At that time

View down over Botton Village.

112

these were all completely new concepts. Parents and co-workers formed the Camphill Village Trust which was to be the vehicle for bringing about the first village community.

Winter in Botton Village.

Many properties were seen, but none of them had the space to accommodate all that would have to be developed. At one meeting, however, Peggy Macmillan, the mother of one of the first children in the Camphill Schools and a close relative of the former Prime Minister Sir Harold Macmillan, suggested that Botton Hall, the family's country estate, might be worth a look as it was too big for the family to use. Dr König and others went to view the hall and its three farms at the head of a valley in the North Yorkshire moors. It was clear that this was the place to start, and with the great generosity of the Macmillan family the first Camphill Village started. In the autumn of 1955 a group of pioneer villagers and co-workers dropped down on the windswept moors to take possession of Botton Hall and its farms.

Today, Botton Village extends over six hundred acres of woodland, farm and horticultural land. It has twenty-seven dwelling houses, a large community centre, six farms, eight workshops, and is involved in supplying an international market with craft goods. The final two years of a eurythmy training is based at Botton, and a therapy unit, Thomas Weihs House, was built to provide care and therapy for ageing villagers and co-workers.

In addition to meeting the requirements for adults in need of special care Botton was, by the mid eighties, acting as an agency offering work to more than a hundred unemployed men, women and school leavers from the area. It is estimated that up to ten thousand visitors come to Botton each year. The Waldorf School which started in 1960 on the perimeter of Botton's land attracts children from outside the village. It has become apparent that the requirement to provide the kind of setting for a beneficial life for those with special needs calls on the involvement of a wider and wider group of people, and that an otherwise isolated moorland valley can become a focus for new social, cultural and economic activity.

Engraving glass, Botton Village.

Grange-Oaklands

The value of what was happening in Botton did not go unnoticed, and three years after its establishment the Grange, a thirty-four-acre estate at Newnham-on-Severn in Gloucestershire was purchased with the help of the Camphill Village Trust. This was intended to be a place for youngsters who had left school, but in 1961 it became an adult community along the lines of Botton. This estate does not lend itself to farming, situated as it is on a steep slope overlooking the River Severn, but with its rich soil and sunny aspect, it is ideal for fruit growing. For many years now it has produced excellent juices and jams from the fruit grown by bio-dynamic husbandry. The Grange has developed a close-knit group of houses, well-established workshops, and also a beautiful hall and a therapy house.

In 1978, nearby Oakland Park with its large mansion house and 150–acre farm was acquired so the work of the Grange could be extended. This acquisition doubled the number of places for villagers and also added farming to the fruit production and processing. Oaklands Park has become a commercial bio-dynamic horticultural enterprise with widespread consumer interest. The work of the villagers is an essential part of the production process and enables them to take a full part in the economic life.

Delrow

Dr König saw many children and adults in need of special care during the early days of Camphill's work in England. In 1950 a London centre was started in Harley Street where, among other activities, Dr König's clinics could be held. In 1963 this centre was transferred to Delrow House, fourteen miles north of London near Watford. Delrow has been the centre for the Camphill Village Trust (CVT) offices, and for the clinics for applicants for CVT places. Delrow consists of a seventeenth-century house, a small estate, workshops and a large hall and college complex. This attracts many visiting artists and hosts conferences and meetings on the work of Camphill and similar organizations. In this way Delrow has always been open and outward looking, acting as a rehabilitation and assessment centre for many individuals, a high proportion of whom have some form of psychiatric disorder.

New directions

In looking back to the beginning of Camphill and the pioneering work in England, we have to note the changing attitude in the Western world towards those with special needs. Dr König's vision 1954 no longer sounds so radical and for this we can be thankful. Also, the development of such children into adult life can be helped in many ways other than in sheltered communities and sheltered workshops.

In 1969 a group of people, many from Botton Village, started **Camphill Houses, Stourbridge**. They wanted to have the opportunity of experiencing life in town, of having an ordinary job and a more independent lifestyle. In the early days jobs were easily found and some held these jobs for many years. Others were able to move on to completely independent living in lodgings or a flat or house of their own. Camphill Houses now consists of four households indistinguishable in appearance from their neighbours, and in walking distance of each other. The complex has become home base for a large number of people, but some may not be seen all week, merely calling on a Saturday to attend the Bible evening.

In 1970 the **Mount School** near Tunbridge Wells in East Sussex began. The founding group had asked Dr Weihs where, from his experience among the young people in his London clinic,

the greatest needs lay. Dr Weihs had described the plight of the twelve to fourteen-year-old who, because of behavioural and other difficulties, had not progressed in other special schools. This group of co-workers took over the Mount, a run-down former Roman Catholic seminary, and transformed it into a place for many of these difficult children, helping them to make their way through the stormy years of adolescence.

The only centre in Wales, **Coleg Elidyr**, began in 1973 in a bleak farmhouse on a hillside overlooking a beautiful valley in the southern Cambrian Mountains. Those who crossed the border into Wales wanted to create a place where it would be obvious to teenagers with special needs that though they had left school at sixteen, just like other youngsters, they could continue their learning, both academically and practically. Coleg Elidyr has since gained recognition for showing that the time from school-leaving to becoming an adult is of critical importance for all young people, particularly so for those with special needs. In Coleg Elidyr, the steps of further education, apprenticeship and journeyman, are marked by different social and educational experiences. The college of further education is based on the main hundred-acre campus; apprenticeship is experienced in a nearby town in three houses, a café, shops and workshops; and the journeyman is trained on a 150–acre farm.

In 1975 **Cherry Orchards** opened in seventeen acres in a densely populated area of Bristol as a non-specialized therapeutic community. It is open to children, adolescents and adults with special needs. It believes in adapting the potential of the place to ongoing needs rather than being a place where people fit into a well-defined framework. This enables Cherry Orchards to take individuals with severe problems who can begin to live and work with others in a constructive way.

Above: Delrow College, Watford, Herts. Below: The Mount, Tunbridge Wells, Sussex. Opposite: Basketry and candle-making workshop.

In 1976 the North Yorkshire market town of Malton became home for the **Croft Community**. In a similar way to the Stourbridge centre, the Croft answered the need of some adults, many coming from Botton, to move from a rural to an urban life. The Croft has established four households in different parts of the town and there is close contact with the busy local community which is helped by an excellent book and coffee shop which the centre has established near the market. Along with the other urban communities, the Croft faces the challenge of being in a community, part of the local surroundings, as well as having an identity which is recognizably Camphill.

A third centre in the North of England is the **Pennine Community**, established in 1977 in the area where the Industrial Revolution started. A large stone house with twenty-four acres of land was bought, and the community started with similar aims to Cherry Orchards: to offer a place of mutual help for many differing needs and ages. By 1981 this changed with a stronger emphasis being put on the needs of adolescents. A college has been built up which provides education, craft work and work on the land. The Pennine Community has also taken over part of an old coal mine and plans to transform this into craft workshops.

The sixth place to be established during the 1970s was **William Morris House**. In the Severn Valley near Stroud and Gloucester, a former workhouse for the destitute (later a home for the elderly) was acquired and extensively modified. The house had very little land, but this was acceptable as there was a desire to build up craft work (as indicated by the name of the community, William Morris, the nineteenth-century craftsman and artist). Later, another house with land was bought a few minutes walk away, and this has provided the possibility of land work to complement the fine craft products that come out of the workshops.

Five of these six places are principally involved in meeting the needs of adolescents, and when they were founded the situation of these young people was of primary concern to those in the English region.

By 1981 the new Education Act for England and Wales recognized that all children, irrespective of ability, should receive education up to school leaving age, and have the option of continuing education up to the age of nineteen. There has been tremendous progress in social-educational understanding in the relatively short time since Camphill began in England. In 1978 the Camphill communities in Britain working with adolescents began meeting together to reach a better understanding of adolescence. From these meetings Centres of Youth Guidance emerged and became a third aspect alongside the schools and communities working with adults. With the Urban Communities, the English-Welsh region now has four ways of meeting the needs of people, be they children, adolescents or adults with special needs.

In 1980 Devon Health Authority approached Camphill to ask for help in providing a Camphill community for some of its long-term psychiatric hospital patients. The policy of closing these hospitals was gaining momentum, but the question remained of how best to safeguard these institutionalized individuals.

With the direct involvement of the county authority, **Hapstead House**, a large, former sanatorium on the edge of Buckfastleigh, was bought and forty people admitted. It was not easy to build a bridge between institutional and community life for these people but with the experience of Botton Village and the presence of some Botton villagers, the process began. Hapstead House soon had its maximum population of 70 people: villagers, co-workers and children.

Milton Keynes Community started a year later, after the Camphill Village Trust was approached by the Milton Keynes Health Authority and the town's development corporation. Milton Keynes is a new town built to take some of the overflow population from London. Despite the existence of various styles of housing, carefully planned road systems and shopping areas, the development corporation felt that an innovative social venture such as offered by Camphill would be urgently needed. Housing was rented from the corporation and co-workers

Opposite: Open day sideshows, Botton Village, Yorkshire.

118

and companions moved into three small family houses which had connecting doors installed to provide common living space. With a small amount of land, a vegetable garden was started, and later a hall and workshops and another site acquired.

Middlesborough in the North-West of England has for many years been a place with one of the highest levels of unemployment in the country, and a reputation for being run down and uninspiring. It is only a few miles north of Botton Village, and a visit by the Middlesborough Town Planning Department led to the question of whether the social, cultural and economic forms that had developed at Botton could be considered in planning for the revitalization of Middlesborough. Larchfield, a 125–acre farm on the outskirts of the town, was leased to Camphill Village Trust by Middlesborough Corporation. **Larchfield Community** began in 1986 with Middlesborough Town Council and Camphill working together to find a common image and a common means of building up a community. This site has provided building, landscaping, farm and horticultural work for special employment schemes for disadvantaged individuals and young offenders. In this setting the adult with special needs becomes not so much the one who requires help but the helper of others, providing the warm and personal contact which oversteps the barriers of "unemployment" and "deprivation".

In 1987 **Thornage Hall,** a thirteenth-century Norfolk village hall, was donated to Camphill answering a request made by parents twenty-five years earlier that Camphill start a village community in East Anglia. Thornage is a venture started as a partial answer to the need for places for the more difficult and less able person who cannot find a place in a working village or urban community.

Looking back over the years and trying to assess the qualities and potential of such a region with its seventeen establishments, it is apparent that the growth of the places has come about as a response to many different needs. In the early days it was the child who required schooling and curative education. Later the village communities appeared providing work and an adult social life. Then came the move from the rural to the urban communities. Through the realization by professional people that communities such as Camphill are able to offer help to a diversity of needs, the places for adolescents could be established.

The involvement with local authorities and the links between the problems of modern social life and the potential for social renewal through community life are forged with the help of those who clearly require our help. Today those who need help are increasingly the people who suffer from a psychiatric illness, or those who, though of normal intelligence, cannot cope with everyday life. There are also those who leave school and are unemployable in the usual sense.

Conclusion

Rudolf Steiner said that the task of England, and this can include the English-speaking world, is to develop the consciousness soul. What does this mean? It is summed up in words from his first Mystery Play:

> In times to come
> Human beings will have
> To exist for one another
> And not the one through the other,
> Thus is reached the World's ultimate aim
> When each one is with themselves
> And each will give to the other
> What none would demand.*

* *The Portal of Initiation,*
Rudolf Steiner

A wedding at Botton Village, Yorkshire. The Camphill Book & Coffee Shop at Malton, Yorkshire (below).

Perhaps this can be understood to mean that each person will have to become more "themselves", to know themselves, but through this to make the other person the focus of concern and attention rather than one's own well-being. This requires going beyond individualism in the search for new forms of social life.

Diversity requires communication if it is not to lead to separation. This makes the English region into a reality as time and again groups and individuals are called together to assess the strengths and weaknesses of the establishments, and to gain insights which are true for all the places involved in the work.

The Irish region

Patrick Lydon

Ireland, the Emerald Isle, land of saints and scholars, Ireland of the Welcomes, the ancient home of the Celtic civilization, is the beautiful green island where Christianity has flourished since the time of St Patrick. Ireland is the most underdeveloped country in Western Europe, politically oppressed for eight hundred years, now a nation divided, where nationalism has fuelled a violent conflict for more than twenty years.

The land of Ireland, both North and South, has welcomed Camphill in a special way, and is now home to six communities which together form one of the seven regions of the Camphill movement. It is a region with a strong sense of cohesion, common activity and mutual support, despite covering two countries which have very different administrative structures, and, in fact, two cultures. Perhaps the creation of this Camphill region can bring together the factions, and create a sense of community and wholeness in this ancient land.

There are three Camphill communities in Northern Ireland, and three, with the beginnings of a fourth, in the Republic. They have all arisen from Glencraig, the first of these centres, which was founded after Dr König met with parents and friends of handicapped children in Belfast in 1953. **Glencraig,** founded in 1954, began as a school on a small estate on the shores

Glencraig near Belfast.

122

of Belfast Lough. As the children grew older, the school grew larger, and Glencraig gradually developed a village community on the same estate. This was the first time that a school and a village had developed in the same community. Later, a training school, a separate programme for the children who left school and needed further education and skills training, was established. Glencraig became a large community with more than two hundred people, a complex internal structure, and a richness that could become the source of many new community impulses.

In 1971 the expanding need for adult places led to the foundation of the **Mourne Grange** village community near Kilkeel, on the south-eastern shore of Northern Ireland. Lying between the sea and the imposing, majestic Mountains of Mourne, on an eighty-acre estate that had been a boarding school, Mourne Grange set out to be a village devoted to working and caring for the land.

Six months later, another new village community began in the Republic. Dublin parents of children at Glencraig found a house on a small farm in County Wexford on the east coast, called **Duffcarrig**, and the first group moved there from Glencraig in February 1972. The Republic is the poorer country, but the new community received enthusiastic and generous support from both government and the people. Perhaps the fact that caring for the handicapped and deprived has traditionally been the responsibility of the religious orders gave Camphill's community approach a special significance. The work of Camphill quickly found a home in the south.

After a period of expansion and consolidation in these new communities, the call came to take up new tasks. A group of parents with autistic children in Dublin asked Camphill to start

The Mourne Mountains behind Mourne Grange, Co Down, Northern Ireland.

Raymond and Geoff,
Mourne Grange.
Ballytobin, Co Kilkenny
(right).

a school for difficult and disturbed children. In 1979, **Ballytobin**, in County Kilkenny, a small farm which grew to become a home and school for handicapped children, was started. Like Glencraig, Ballytobin also included a number of handicapped adults.

In the north, in spite of the rapid development of Mourne Grange, there was still a demand for more places for handicapped adults, and in 1984, Camphill acquired a farm at **Clanabogan** in County Tyrone. Clanabogan was the first step to the west; to a rural area with deeply ingrained sectarian divisions. But the ground had been well prepared and Clanabogan soon established itself as a small, land-working village, its non-denominational caring work bringing an element of healing to the surrounding community.

With Ballytobin becoming firmly established, there again arose the need for more adult places in the south. For several years the supporters of Camphill had hoped for a development around Dublin, the country's capital, and in 1985 a community was founded at **Dunshane**, near Naas in County Kildare, not far from Dublin. Dunshane took up the task of training adolescents and young adults for mature adulthood.

A very different process led to the creation of another community. A group of people in a parish near Ballytobin asked whether it would be possible to start a home for the handicapped people in their area. Discussions on how best to do this took place over several years, and local people searched for a suitable home for this work. Late in 1986 a thirty-eight-acre farm at Temple Michael, **Grangemockler**, in County Tipperary, was bought and the house renovated for occupation late in 1988. This is the first facility for mentally handicapped adults in the whole of South Tipperary, and stands as an expression of the social concern and commitment of the rural community at Grangemockler.

Nearly forty years after the founding of Glencraig, the work of Camphill has created seven communities in Ireland. These seven places give a varied and complex expression to many aspects of the Camphill impulse. **Glencraig** is one of the large and mature communities of the

Camphill movement; one of the communities that give the movement a sense of its history. So many children have come to the school, made a deep impression on the many people who have cared for and taught them, and have grown up to become the responsible adults who carry new communities. Hundreds of young people have come to Glencraig and completed the seminar in curative education.

Glencraig continues to develop and change. After years of the village being integrated with the school community, and with the training school having its own life in the midst of this large community, the complexity of the arrangements became too much to maintain. the decision was made to concentrate on two impulses: curative education and bio-dynamic agriculture. It was felt that the village impulse should gradually move out to the other villages in Northern Ireland. A new young adults training scheme met the needs of the young people leaving the training school, and, bearing in mind new government education regulations, the community has put extra strength into the school life.

The sense of purpose of the village impulse has guided the steady development of **Mourne Grange**. It aims to uphold the dignity of the individual through meaningful work, genuine human relationships and mindfulness of spirit. From the beginning the young community took up work on the land with great enthusiasm. The old boarding school cricket pitch was ploughed and planted with strawberries. Old houses were transformed and new ones built. As the community grew, attention turned to the craft workshops. Pottery, weaving, woodwork and baking all became part of life at Mourne Grange, and goods of the highest quality were produced. A craft and coffee shop were built which brought more contact with the surrounding community.

Dunshane, Co Kildare.

Farming has something for everyone. Early morning milking at Mourne Grange and Glencraig.

After years of hard work and constant expansion and development, Mourne Grange is branching out from a strong foundation. Now the task is to light the flame of cultural life. A Christian Community priest lives in the community and can serve its spiritual needs, as well as travelling to other centres in the region. There are the solid beginnings of a village school to provide for the educational needs of the co-workers' children. An architect of the Camphill

Architects Group, which designs buildings for centres in all regions of the movement, has come to work and live in Mourne Grange, and will oversee the construction of the new hall.

Clanabogan, after three years of concentrated preparation, entered its first stage of rapid growth. Numbers doubled from thirty to sixty souls, three new households were completed and new workshops built. The future of Clanabogan is very open. The community is holding discussions with the local health and social services board about providing opportunities for day employment of local people, perhaps integrating their services with a nearby training workshop.

Glencraig, Mourne Grange and Clanabogan in the North work together with a remarkable spirit. After years of each community facing its development and struggles alone, the communities have come to a common vision of Camphill's development in Northern Ireland and are helping each other to achieve their goals. The government makes strong administrative demands on the communities, and each of them must comply with strict regulations. But when these demands are fulfilled, the support of the government has been generous. On the basis of rigorous budgeting, the centres are now able to create a fund for capital projects.

The quality of life in the South is very different. While the social fabric of the Republic of Ireland has not been torn apart by the conflicts that have divided Northern Ireland, the economy is considerably less developed and affluent. The country was never industrialized. It is predominantly rural and has remained true to its strong religious traditions. Unhampered by the strict regulations of a modern welfare state, Camphill has met a country where money is scarce but where moral support is given generously. Development has come less through careful planning than through the spontaneous initiative of parents and friends who wanted to find a place for their relatives who needed care.

Duffcarrig, founded in 1972, is now a mature village community with eighty-five people, but a village with its own distinctive character. It has cultivated an attitude of acceptance that has made it possible to integrate many difficult people into the community. Many of the villagers are quite severely handicapped. Many do not speak or are not socially responsive and cannot work out of their own motivation. It is a strong challenge to create a vital community with many people who are not able to participate in an active way. For many years Duffcarrig had no place where the whole community can comfortably be together and a great effort is being made to build a hall that will enhance the remarkable therapeutic impulse that lives there.

The therapeutic impulse is also central to the life at **Ballytobin**. Now a community of sixty souls, Ballytobin set out to make a home for children with a wide range of handicaps, and to create a life that would stimulate and nourish them. A therapeutic farm was evolved, in which the natural rhythms of rural life and work on the land are the background for a curative approach to children who had been unable to fit into the world around them. Only gradually did the school develop, but it is now an integral part of the community's life.

In order to keep a healthy relationship with the rural character of the community, Ballytobin hoped to remain a small community and to foster a style of development that would lead to a local network of smaller communities, each having its own purpose and character. As the first children grew towards adulthood, there was a long search for a suitable place to create a sister community nearby. In 1987, a small farm was purchased at **Kyle**, three miles away. This is gradually becoming the new growth point where the children who have grown up in Ballytobin, and many others, will make their adult lives.

The new community at **Grangemockler** will also be part of this local grouping of communities. The old farmhouse, vacant for fifty-three years, has been renovated and extended, and a new house will soon be under construction.

Dunshane has a different quality to Duffcarrig or Ballytobin. The young people are generally more capable than those in the other two places, but their special problems are social deprivation

Ballytobin, Co Kilkenny.

and maladjustment. Dunshane offers higher education where ideas and art and creative work are brought to young people who have been deprived of ideals and security and moral values. As in other centres, there is a huge demand for places. Dunshane houses sixty people, and a number of local people come on a day basis.

Ireland, both north and south, has proved fertile ground for the work of the Camphill movement. One can wonder why this small country has seen such a steady and harmonious development of Camphill, and why there is continuing demand for places in every centre.

In Ireland the conflict between traditional Christian faith and the challenge of modern materialism is particularly poignant. In the midst of the sectarian conflict in the North, and in the challenge to the authority of the religious and moral tradition in the South, there is a yearning for an inspired Christianity that will show the way into the future. An important underlying aspect of Camphill is the attempt to discover a renewed Christianity; to put into practice a Christian devotion that can bind together a new understanding of nature, art and science, of personal motivation and social organization, through the individual's striving to respond to the need of his fellow human being, inspired by Christian love.

This aspect of Camphill has a definite place in the landscape of Irish life.

128

The Central European region

Hans Müller-Wiedemann

As in the United States and South Africa, Camphill's work in Germany began in the 1950s. The Camphill impulse, which originated in Austria, returned again to Central Europe. Preceded by many consultations to determine the demand for Camphill in Germany, it was also apparent that Dr König wished to bring the ideas of Camphill to fruition in Germany, as these ideals seemed related to the destiny or potential of Central Europe. So in 1958 a small group of co-workers started in **Brachenreuthe** near Überlingen on the Lake of Constance to work with severely handicapped, cerebral palsied and speech-impaired children.

Dr König visited regularly, and then took up residence in Brachenreuthe in 1964 together with Alix Roth, his secretary and assistant. Dr König experienced the activity related to old Central European spirituality: the early Christianizing of the landscape through the devout work of Celtic monks and the influence of the medieval mystics. In addition to curative education, the husbandry of the earth and land belonged to the central impulses of Camphill at the Lake Constance. Eberhard Schicker, a professional colleague of Dr König, helped to inaugurate Camphill's work in Germany.

Brachenreuthe, once described as the Camphill movement's dearest child, was deeply influenced by Dr König's charismatic and powerful personality. Requests for admission grew dramatically, and a second centre soon became necessary. A new residential school, Föhrenbühl, was founded nearby, and in 1966 another in Bruckfelden. Positive contacts with colleagues in

Outing from Humanus Haus, Bernese Oberland, Switzerland (below). Opposite: Learning to write.

View from Brachenreuthe School, Lake Constance, Germany.

the wider curative education movement were soon established. With the expanding school work the idea of a village grew, inspired primarily by Dr König's extensive lecturing and the initiative of parents of older handicapped children. Government and local authorities were open to new developments. After a first attempt in Brachenreuthe the village idea took root at the **Lehenhof**, an estate near the Lake Constance in 1964. This was followed twelve years later by a second village community, **Hermannsberg**. In 1987 the **Hausenhof** Village Community was established in close collaboration with the **Karl König School** at Nürnberg, Germany.

As the Camphill Movement grew it was formed into regional groupings. Together with a council of delegates, Karl König assumed responsibility for the different centres within the Central European region. The co-workers of **Aigues-Vertes** and **St Prex**, two places in Switzerland on Lake Geneva, had asked to be associated with, or to join, the Camphill movement. Thus, to begin with, the newly founded region was centred round the lakes of Constance and Geneva.

Until Dr König's death in March 1966 the curative educational and medical therapeutic impulses were firmly rooted within the schools. The village idea had also come to realization, relating curative education with agricultural work and new social forms of living together in community.

Karl König inspired the work not only from within the circle of co-workers, but also shared his ideas with a much larger circle of people by public lecturing. Here he spoke about the concept of the human being as seen in anthroposophical curative education and about some of the fundamental ideas of the Camphill movement.

During these first years, four pillars of residential curative educational work were formed and established: therapeutic efforts for the individual child; the educational work of the teachers' college and the whole area of schooling; the daily care of the children within their residential house communities; and thorough medical supervision. During this time the care for movement-disturbed, speech-impaired and autistic children stood in the foreground.

Dr König had made plans to visit East Germany, Hungary and Czechoslovakia, as it seemed possible that Camphill could be established in Eastern Europe. However, he died before this could happen.

The Central European region began to spread towards the west. **Christophorus**, a centre in Zeist, Holland, became affiliated, and in 1977 the first Camphill community in France, **Le Béal**, in Provence, was founded. In 1973 the Karl König School in Nürnberg became the first non-residential Camphill school. In 1975 **Thomas House** was established in Berlin, caring for pre-school children.

130

In the same year in Vienna, Austria, an association was formed which, a year later, began to build a village community in **Liebenfels**, in Carinthia.

For nearly twenty years, co-workers from all the Central European region centres have been meeting annually in Beitenwil, Switzerland, to help ensure that the region stays "alive and vital". These meetings focus on Rudolf Steiner's ideas concerning renewal of the social organism (the threefold social order) as well as its implications for the various Camphill communities. In addition, co-workers meet regularly in three different councils, which consider human concerns and the legal and rights life, the formation of co-operative associations in the economic sphere, and the cultural life (or spiritual life). These three councils have superseded the original council of delegates and address questions and concerns the co-workers have, both as individuals and arising out of their experiences in the centres. Many of these questions relate to the development of the social structure and experience of community living.

To attempt to develop an awareness of the three spheres of social life as enumerated by Rudolf Steiner, and to bring them into the life of the community was a strong impulse of the Central European region which soon spread to the other regions of the Camphill movement. Meetings to consider these questions with delegates from the various regions, now take place regularly.

Humanus Haus community with view of Bernese Oberland.

Everyone helps collecting hay at Brachenreuthe, Lake Constance, Germany (below).

These questions, of course, arise in a certain social situation. As well as the authorities and representatives of other organizations working with the handicapped, there is also the Anthroposophical Society and its different initiatives, and the large circle of parents and friends. In Germany, Freundeskreis Camphill (Friends of Camphill) was founded in 1965. In a letter sent by Dr König to the parents who were to found this organization he wrote: "Our children are not only here so that we may help them, but that we are being helped by them. It is a giving and taking; a power may arise, rare today, and one we all seem to lose, which, however, is most important in human relationships: trust in the other human being and trust in the spiritual world."

A yearly parents' conference deepens the relationship between the schools, the villages and the parents. Since the early 1970s, Camphill's relationship to other curative education schools and villages in Central Europe has also been strengthened. In 1979, co-workers of the Central European region helped establish the Conference of Curative Education and Social Therapy at the Goetheanum in Dornach, Switzerland. In regular meetings of this body, and in other such groupings nationally, relationships within the whole of the curative movement have been considerably strengthened.

Training and craft workshops, Föhrenbühl, Germany.

School and village communities in Germany

The concentration of Camphill centres at Lake Constance created a wider social organism in which common aspects of the work could be discussed in meetings of the schools and villages, and in a joint adult education training course in curative education and social therapy. In 1979, the co-workers in the area developed new statutes in which the aims of Camphill regarding the new social endeavour of living with people in need of special care could find legal expression.

The curative educational and social-therapeutic work of Camphill in Germany started in **Brachenreuthe**. In time, the work became centred around the needs of the autistic child, and by the beginning of the 1970s the child population had reached ninety.

When the school at Brachenreuthe reached its capacity **Föhrenbühl**, twenty kilometres away was purchased. In the past twenty-five years it has undergone many developments. There are now thirteen house communities with 118 children and young people, twenty day pupils and thirty-seven children and young people come from Bruckfelden each day. There is a nursery class for handicapped and non-handicapped staff children.

Föhrenbühl has established a training school for youngsters from Brachenreuthe, Bruckfelden and Föhrenbühl which, as well as classroom space, has eleven workshops.

Karl König initiated **Adalbert Stifter House**, near Bruckfelden and between Brachenreuthe and Föhrenbühl, early in 1966, so that work with autistic children could begin.

Many conferences take place at Föhrenbühl: speech therapists have annual conferences, classroom teachers meet regularly, and, recently, physicians working in the Camphill movement have started meeting at Lake Constance. From the beginning medical care has played an important part and this is apparent in further education, the regular child study meetings and in clinical demonstrations and studies. In-service courses for curative teachers take place each year, and since 1982 an eighteen-month course qualifies students who have completed a curative training to work with curative eurythmy.

Brachenreuthe, Föhrenbühl and Bruckfelden offer a four-year adult training course in curative education, and some eighty students from all over the world are participating in this college.

The **Lehenhof** Village Community was founded by Dr König in September 1964, and is the oldest Camphill village in Germany. Lehenhof has grown and is now a village-like settlement with workshops and house communities. As well as the workshops which produce crafts such

School (above) and Community Hall (tope right and below) at Föhrenbühl, Lake Constance, Germany.

as weaving and spinning, there is a bakery selling bread over a wide area; a workshop manufacturing woollen underwear and pullovers; and a sawmill and factory producing large numbers of wooden fruit boxes. Agriculture and market gardening has been important from the start, for the care of the land goes hand in hand with the care a social organism requires. Following what Rudolf Steiner stated to be the fundamental social law, the individual's need for money is not bound to his work productivity. The income from the sale of products contributes to everyone's living, thereby reducing the fees paid by the authorities.

A hospital with maternity ward, consulting and therapy rooms has been established, and suitable accommodation and care for the aged is being offered. The community has expanded into the valley below, buying houses in the local village.

In 1976 an old monastery with a chapel and other buildings close to the hamlet of Hattenweiler, also near Lake Constance, was bought. Here the **Hermannsberg** Village Community was founded housing 150 people, of whom eighty require special care. There are twelve households with from two to eight villagers living in them. Basket making, weaving, knitting and spinning workshops, as well as a joinery, woodwork shop and school exercise book production offer many different work possibilities. There is also a large laundry which services the other Camphill centres.

In 1973, work with pre-school children began in Nürnberg. This grew into a nursery school in 1975, and later became the **Karl König School**, the first day-centre in the Camphill movement. From the start, a very fruitful co-operation with the parents ensured the growth of the school.

Following the untiring efforts of co-workers, parents and friends of the Nürnberg school, the ancient and isolated **Hausenhof** farmhouse sixty kilometres west of the city was bought in 1983, and in 1985 bio-dynamic farming started. The Hausenhof Village Community offers a home and work to about twenty people.

Curative education began in Berlin in 1975 when a psychiatric-neurological consultant wished to relate to the curative educational and social impulses of Camphill. Supported by parents, a day centre for speech-impaired pre-school children was founded. In this centre, the **Thomas House** for Curative Education and Speech Therapy, a wide range of therapies are offered for about forty young children. Regular in-service courses are held there, particularly for nurses, as there has been a trend of training experienced curative teachers for nursing in Camphill.

134

Le Béal, northern Provence, France.

France

Le Béal Community near the Rhône began in 1977 following a request from a family farming with handicapped people who wished to pass on their responsibility. In the midst of Provence, influenced by the Mediterranean climate, with the air enriched by the scent of many herbs, and imbued with the light that inspired Cezanne and Van Gogh, the community began its work in a large house. During the French Revolution silk had been produced there, an activity directly promoted by the Count of St Germain. Le Béal is recognized by the French authorities as providing new social forms of living and working with people in need of special care. Work on the land and care for plants, shrubs and trees form the core of the work for the community. The small community feels related to the Camphill centres in the French-speaking part of Switzerland, as well as to the expanding anthroposophical curative educational work in France.

Holland

Christophorus, in Zeist, in the middle of Holland, was founded in 1953. In February that year there was a heavy flood, a terrifying event, as much of the country lies below sea level, and the founding group had witnessed the way people helped each other. This group formed a committee called the League for Social, Pedagogical and Therapeutic Impulses. They started by opening a house to care for maladjusted children, and later other houses were acquired, forming an urban community within the larger community. From the beginning the co-workers worked to transform the sandy soil by planting trees and cultivating gardens.

Christophorus formed close links to the Irish region of the Camphill movement in the early days, aided by regular working visits from Dr Hans Heinrich Engel from Glencraig, whose initiative brought about a three-year music therapy course in Holland. Today, there are sixty children attending the school, and about thirty young people studying in the training school. There are many anthroposophical activities in the immediate surroundings, including a teachers' college, a therapy college, and a Waldorf school, as well as an independent university. Good relations have been established with the other curative homes and the training course in curative education works in close co-operation with the other anthroposophical institutions.

On the island of Texel the village impulse has found a home in **Het Maartenhuis**, founded in 1980. This small centre, which enriches the cultural life of the island, is to be enlarged to form a village community. In the western part of Holland another initiative has also started.

Switzerland

Just above the small town of St Prex on Lake Geneva, twenty-two kilometres west of Lausanne, and surrounded by vineyards, is the Centre de Pédagogie Curative **Perceval**. This Camphill community has expanded from an organization offering residential special school to one providing living and working opportunities for handicapped adults.

Founded in 1951 as a curative educational home, Perceval joined the Camphill movement in 1965. It is constituted as a trust in which parents and co-workers are jointly represented. There are about fifty-five children and thirty-three adults in need of special care in residence. Three of the houses are outside Perceval, with one of the family units right in the centre of St Prex running a shop which sells community produce as well as newspapers and general goods. The Perceval school offers a full twelve years' schooling. Gardens and farm are run on bio-dynamic principles and form an important part of the community.

The community has been instrumental in extending the work of the Camphill movement and other anthroposophical endeavours in the area: a eurythmy training was accommodated and this initiative has gone on to establish itself independently as the Eurythmée in Lausanne, and the Waldorf school in Lausanne/Morges began as a first class for staff children in Perceval.

With Aigues Vertes, Perceval has, since 1977, formed an important link to other curative education centres in France, especially through its participation in the Cercle de Liaison for anthroposophical curative education and social therapy within the French-speaking area. Perceval's Camphill college offers a three-year training course in curative education and a course in social therapy.

In 1961 the first president of the Foundation **Aigues Vertes** gave this name, which means green water, to a new village near the Rhône which still carries green water. Aigues Vertes is on a large curve of the river near the French border just downstream from Lake Geneva.

From the start, parents and friends of the Foundation Aigues Vertes played an important role, giving their support in developing the village. An assembly hall serves the needs of community life, and in the chapel the Sunday service can be celebrated.

Since 1975 The Christian Community's Act of Consecration of Man has been regularly celebrated. The Aigues Vertes community has helped to establish the work of The Christian Community at Lake Geneva and has given active patronage to a new Waldorf school nearby.

Next to running the workshops and farm, the life of the village centres around the care for the more severely disabled people.

At Michaelmas 1978 a three-year course in social therapy in the French language was started, the first such undertaking in the Romance countries.

The impulse which led to the founding of **Humanus House** grew out of experiences gained in curative education work at Perceval. Humanus House started in 1973 within a farming area near Berne between Lake Geneva and Lake Constance. The community offers sixty handicapped people a social and working life, and for thirty-five youths there is craft training as well as

View from Perceval, St Prex, to Lake Geneva, Switzerland.

schooling to prepare them for integration into society. One workshop builds Choroi harps as well as solo and soprano lyres.

In Humanus House, which takes its name from the central figure in Goethe's poem *Die Geheimnisse* (the Mysteries), a great deal is done in further education and artistic activities, particularly for the young apprentices in the training school.

Alongside the trust council, an association of friends and parents, with more than 650 members, actively participate in the life and development of the community.

Austria*

Austria is the "birthplace" of Anthroposophy, and also of Camphill, but it had to wait until 1976 for the establishment of its first Camphill endeavour. One may wonder why it took so long for Camphill to find its way back to its "homeland", having been established for so long in other countries. Perhaps this shows that Camphill, although of Central European origin, is independent of geographical and national boundaries and can find a home in any country where it is needed.

Camphill **Liebenfels** is about twenty-five kilometres north of Klagenfurt in the beautiful and harmonious landscape of the Carinthian heartland. The southern part of Austria has a rich cultural and historical heritage. The Celts came to the area in the fifth century BC. Many archaeological findings bear witness to this, among them a Celtic temple dedicated to the goddess Isis Norea in Liebenfels. The Celts were succeeded by the Romans, who also left a strong imprint. It was only in the eighth century that Austria became Christianized, but the Roman Catholic church remains strong.

Liebenfels comprises four settlements, Wertsch, Mossenig, Quellenhof and Pflausach, spread out with from two to eight kilometres between them. The six households live mainly in converted farm houses and house about a hundred people, just over half of them with mental retardation. There is a large wood-workshop in Mossenig producing garden furniture, toys and napkin rings. There is also a woollen and silk workshop producing underwear which provides both work and much needed income. The weaving shop gives work to many in Wertsch, and in Pflausach a bakery caters for the needs of all the settlements producing bread, cakes, biscuits, pizzas, and mixed cereals, as well as selling to an increasing number of outside customers. The farmers on the two small farms use horses instead of tractors.

Only Pflausach is owned, the other three places being rented. Austria is a relatively poor country, and the income is correspondingly low, making for a perpetual shortage of money. However, again and again at crucial moments generous help has been given by other Camphill centres. Without this help, Liebenfels could not have developed. There are plans to develop Pflausach, which is most beautifully situated at a height of 850 metres with a splendid view over the valley below, and the Karawanken Mountains of Yugoslavia.

A simple but lovely assembly hall seating 120 has been built at Pflausach in a converted outbuilding. Quite a variety of cultural activities take place there, and they are increasingly attracting a growing number of visitors from the surrounding area.

The Austrian character has no doubt influenced the way of life in Liebenfels, and given it a certain colouring. Yet in the large family of Camphill centres, Liebenfels has found a place and endeavours to make its contribution.

Workshops at Humanus Haus, Switzerland. Herb-drying (top), woodwork-shop (centre and lower), instrument making (opposite).

* This contribution is written by Marianne Sander.

General outlook

Liebenfels, Carinthia, Austria (above). Humanus Haus, Bernese Oberland, Switzerland (below).

Within the past few years, the centres in Germany, France, Holland, Austria and Switzerland have made efforts to relate more directly to their own surroundings, and to seek co-operation with other endeavours. One of the things which characterizes this region is the work of the different councils with the threefold social organism. There is no central management or legal structure relating to the region as a whole.

The Central European region, through communication and co-operation, attempts to uphold the basic and fundamental aims of Camphill. Efforts to re-enliven the social impulses which Rudolf Steiner inaugurated in 1918–19 have been important. In this region Camphill feels itself united with other anthroposophical efforts and within the past three years these efforts have born fruit in building up associations in the economic sphere between producers.

The methods and content of the many adult education training courses and further education given in this region ask to be constantly reviewed.

The members of the different college faculties meet annually in Perceval for mutual exchange. In the past years our outer development has taken second place to our need to give space to deepen and differentiate the methods of working and striving within Camphill.

While many people have been vitally engaged in creating the Camphill movement in Central Europe, Alix Roth must be mentioned with gratitude. From the very beginning she accompanied the destiny of the region until her death in 1987. With quiet awareness of the essentials of life she helped to bring a living relationship to the anthroposophical movement and The Christian Community. She was intimately engaged in fostering the connection between individuals and the centres of the region. As one of the founding members of Camphill she was in an exemplary manner able to build bridges to the younger generation which has had to take increasing responsibility for the life and well-being of the Central European region.

The Scandinavian region

Ivan Jacobsen, Eric Kaufman

Norway

Visitors are shocked to see dragons' heads adorning the ridgepoles of Norway's twelfth-century stave churches. They look as though they are still roaring defiance at King Olav's "White Christ". Christianity came late to Norway, and at the time of the First Crusade its uncertain roots had been in place a mere hundred years. Families of the former Vikings lived well separated from each other; "never less than a stone's throw," as an old adage recounts. Today they still live separated and there are less than twelve people to the square kilometre in a violent and grandiose landscape studded with strange pockets of the past. Flinty and hard, the community concept familiar to peoples further south is seldom experienced. In fact, the Norwegian word for villages applies to villages abroad for in Norway there are no villages.

What was it then that prompted the founding of a Camphill village in such a forbidding landscape? Perhaps it was a need that called for an act of will; and of faith which saw in people and country elements that pointed to the future. The authorities, for their part, probably saw a great deal less. They approved the project, but did little more. Funds to get it off the

Hogganvik village on the fjord, Vikedal, Norway.

The Andreas chapel, Vidaråsen village, Andebu, Norway.

ground had to be found elsewhere. And here the guiding powers intervened swiftly and miraculously in the form of three thousand high school students. Traditionally, Oslo's matriculants devote a day each autumn to a selected social undertaking, and Camphill's Vidaråsen, then only a few weeks old and with nothing more to show than a miserable farm and a glorious idea, was selected from scores of applicants. The village made candles and the students sold them, and a year later the first new family house stood completed. Each year afterwards, for fourteen years, students from Oslo and nearby towns built a new house or a workshop, from the proceeds of candle sales, until today at **Vidaråsen** alone, more than 150 people are together building a community. Of all Camphill's many places, this is perhaps the only one raised by the country's students, some of whom stayed on to become co-workers.

But miracles are rare. A few years later when Camphill sought to sink roots in the "dark mainland" of western Norway, there were few miracles in sight, and the welcome mat was wanting. Here, the physical and spiritual landscape was quite different. There is perhaps no other country where nature plays a greater role in shaping thinking and temperament, which can vary from one valley to the next.

Hogganvik Village lies deep in a fjord with mountains rising steeply from the water. It is an ideal place for trolls and the like. It took three years of ceaseless struggle before Camphill was found sufficiently "non-toxic" to be permitted a foothold here. Struggle indeed, when neighbours were warned that Anthroposophy was nothing less than the Christian clothing assumed by the Antichrist. But even here, distance changed into curiosity, then to hints of grudging admiration and the familiar question, "How do you make it work?"

142

Brass band, Vidaråsen. Water transport and Windmill power at Vallersund Gård, northern Norway.

The history of the **Jøssåsen** Village is completely different. Certainly the most northerly of Camphill's villages, it is near the end of a road leading to the high tundra, on about the same latitude as Yellowknife in Canada's Northwest Territories. Neighbours welcomed anyone willing to share their breathtaking but brief summers, and bleak long winters, and the village soon developed such ties with the community that it is difficult to say where it ends and the neighbourhood begins.

Vallersund, the fourth of Norway's villages, is unique in that it stands as an answer to an invitation. The South Trondelag county played host, and pioneering here had backing and appreciation from the start. Co-workers, villagers and narcotics patients moved in and transformed a picturesque but dilapidated nineteenth-century fishing centre into the most unusual village of them all. Gathering fish and blue mussels for the other villages, it also produces electricity, harnessing the winds roaring in off the North Sea to turn the ninety-foot blades of its wind generator. There are no school children at Vallersund, but, with the nearest Waldorf school more than two hours away by boat, there are plans for a local school. Co-workers children in all the Camphill establishments apart from Vidaråsen have to travel for more than two hours every day to attend school.

Solborg-Alm, a centre for young delinquents established in the mid 1970s lies high up on a mountainside commanding sweeping views of the valley below, and ridge after ridge of blue mountains. Open to the sky it forms a strong contrast to the claustrophobic feeling of Hogganvik. Yet here also the locals showed little enthusiasm for the project. Rich farm land, they thought, should be used for other things, and there was resentment to "hungry foreign interests". But relations improved until a few years later when the Village Trust bought the

Fishing, a primary occupation at Vallersund Gård, Norway. Opposite: Midwinter and summer clearing at Solborg-Alm, Jevnaker, Norway. Vallersund Gård, Norway in summer (bottom right).

neighbouring Alm farm. The sceptics could then nod and mutter "I told you so". Considerable drama ensued. Alm became a village, and shortly afterwards Solborg and Alm joined together so that the villagers might provide an environment in which all the problems and disorder the delinquents brought with them could be dealt with. Implementing this idea, however, is demanding a deep and searching review of Camphill fundamentals.

Today in Norway the word "landsby" (village) is practically synonymous with Camphill thanks to the many books, articles, television programmes and films on the work, but above all to respect for a job well done. Special legislation has been passed enabling Camphill to work unhindered by bureaucracy, and establishing, to quote the law of the land, that the villages are "special care institutions where it is of prime importance that they may operate according to their anthroposophical intentions". Vidaråsen has pioneered a village training course now starting its twentieth year. Neighbours have been sending their children to a Waldorf kindergarten at Solborg-Alm for the past two years, and a Waldorf school will open there shortly. Professor Nils Christie of Oslo University calls the villages "the most exciting social experiment in decades".

As if in defying dragons, distance, and pockets of the past, the villages stand there, and within them people are learning to live together in community. The surroundings are becoming more aware, and as long as they continue to ask, "How do you make it work?" the villages in Norway are on their way to becoming Norwegian villages.

144

Sweden

Sweden's only Camphill village, **Staffansgården** Camphill Community, is about five years old, but its beginnings go back a lot further. Stella Helström and family returned from a year in Camphill Scotland in 1955, and attempted unsuccessfully to plant the village impulse in the Stockholm area. They had to settle for a curative home and school, but a separate unit for youngsters branched off and, after a long period of preparation, was established in Delsbo, a village near the Bosnian Gulf, in 1974.

Delsbo proved to be a good choice. The locals were tolerant and friendly, and nature peaceful with deep forests and quiet lakes. Centuries ago, a pilgrims' route leading to Nidaros Cathedral in Trondheim crossed the Dellen, and there was considerable traffic to and from Russia and farther east.

From the start the initiative had to contend with a government policy which was moving steadily towards the total integration and complete elimination of private care units and homes. Parents and old friends in the Stockholm administration had to work hard to convince the central authorities that the new venture should be granted private status.

During this period, contact with Camphill was strengthened through Peter Roth and friends in Norway and Finland. Bjarne Edberg, The Christian Community priest in Jarna, came regularly, and the Act of Consecration was first held in 1974. Bjarne Edberg was familiar with the work of Camphill in both Scotland and Ireland and proved of immense help in shaping the social structure in preparation for Staffansgården's entry in 1983 into the community of Camphill villages.

In 1981 a farm three kilometres away, **Mickelsgården**, was purchased to provide a training for adults in agriculture and gardening. There is close co-operation between the two establishments and the villagers and trainees have a lot of contact with each other in the interests of strengthening the community concept.

From the start in 1974, the educational-school impulse has been strong. A nursery school was started, and then in 1983 a Waldorf school for normal children. School authorities became interested in a model where handicapped individuals and school children from the neighbourhood could meet and learn about each other's lives. Co-operation between school and town has been most positive and the hot lunches for forty children are prepared with the help of the local inhabitants. All share in the celebration of the festivals, and recently teachers from the school have held courses in Waldorf education with the backing of the University of Sweden.

Perhaps the most telling indication of Camphill's successful integration with its surroundings in Sweden can be seen in the reaction to it of the authorities. Legislation passed in 1987 required all private homes for the mentally handicapped to close. Anthroposophical institutions throughout the country were ordered to close, and the mentally handicapped were to be integrated into society. Camphill Staffansgården, however, was a special case: "We consider your institution to be already integrated," the authorities said. Located in the centre of Delsbo, with co-workers and villagers living together, this first Swedish Camphill centre is integrated with its surroundings in a way that meets the requirements of even the most exacting legislation.

Finland

Camphill in Finland began in 1956 with the establishment of **Sylvia-Koti**, a small curative home, by Carita Stenback. In the mid 1960s Freddy and Kaarina Heimsch arrived to begin work, and in 1970 Sylvia-Koti was reconstituted as a Camphill school. In 1975 **Tapola**, a village community, was founded. Today there are 120 children and adolescents in Sylvia-Koti,

Opposite: Winter sun (top), and spring Sylvia Koti, Lahti, Finland.

Eurythmy (left), and art exhibition at Sylvia Koti, Lahti, Finland.

and Tapola is home to forty villagers. Altogether there are 250 people living in the two establishments, with many others, board and council members, friends and parents, involved. Many young people came to work and live in the two places for either short or long periods, perhaps to take part in the three-year curative education training course or one-year art course at Sylvia-Koti, or the introduction to social therapy course at Tapola.

In the twenty years since Camphill became established in Finland, state social services have greatly improved, and the need for private initiatives to care for the handicapped has decreased. Many private initiatives have disappeared, but Camphill has grown, due largely to the growing interest and activity of parents who want to give alternative care in a community setting to their children. Camphill is a special case, recognized in law, and its existence is guaranteed.

More recent developments have focused on education. Responsibility for the education of the handicapped child is vested in the state, but as a result of negotiations, Sylvia-Koti, while recognized as a state school, is autonomous. All pedagogical, educational and administrative questions remain the responsibility of the teachers, and financial concerns reside with a board.

Sylvia-Koti has recently built a large community centre with a spacious hall and room for therapeutic activities. Many public activities have taken place there, including art exhibitions, theatre, eurythmy and orchestral performances, and conferences. One of the aims of the centre is to bring society and handicapped people closer together.

In this region there is the breath-taking landscape of Norway, with its plunging fjords and spectacular mountains where rock and water meet, and in contrast the quiet and gentle Finnish landscape. In Norway man perches on rock, exposed to nature and the elements. In Finland man is sheltered in a comfortable nest, always surrounded by trees. Perhaps the Camphill establishments are a reflection of the landscape: in Finland there is a school for children; while in Norway the work is with adults. Fittingly, Sweden's Camphill work began by focusing on youngsters facing the transition from adolescence to adulthood.

Even though the region is divided by water and language, co-operation has been strong, and there is regular contact. If you visit Vidaråsen in Norway you may meet some Finnish villagers, or if you are in Tapola you may come across some Swedish villagers, for there are a number of exchanges and visits.

148

The North American region

Andrew Hoy

North America is a land rich in contrasts and contradictions. It is also a land where an idea can be embraced, explored and forgotten with great speed; where there is a "fast food service" for the mind. This speediness is a force to be reckoned with for it provides the possibility for franchises to exist; quick copies.

It is little wonder then that the growth of the Camphill movement in North America has been slow since its inception in 1959. However, it has been a mature and steady growth. Curative education and therapy, as expressed in the work of Camphill, continues to earn respect, but not to make waves. One of our principle tasks is to provide a mirror, and to offer alternatives to prevailing trends, particularly when it appears that everyone embraces a single policy. There cannot be a singular approach to the social problems surrounding those who are labelled as retarded, except to remove the label.

There are seven Camphill centres in North America, providing a home and social life for six hundred souls. Of these, about 270 could be called retarded, a hundred are the children of co-workers, and the remainder are co-workers, seminarists and employees. All the centres — the school at Beaver Run, the training centres of Triform and Soltane, and the four communities for adults — have adopted the social form of the village community. However, the concept of the village community has disappeared from our industrialized society. Already at the beginning of the century the decay of rural life in the United States had become so apparent that a presidential commission was set up by Theodore Roosevelt to study it, and yet the disappearance of village communities continues. Here we find the context for the foundation of the Camphill village life. This form, once appreciated, can be valuable in many ways: bringing soul into a housing development or a sense of purpose into economic enterprise.

The farm complex in early fall at Copake, New York.

In the Camphill village, life unfolds through the interplay of work on the land (farming, gardening, orchard and estate work), work in a variety of craft shops, and work in the household. The expression of a single social form in the Camphill centres of North America is, perhaps, as close as we come to the well-known franchise concept. It may appear to be a limitation of the width of the possible expression of the Camphill idea, and yet it has, in some ways, begun to further the impulse that it serves.

The principle difference between the American centres — each is governed by an independent board of directors — is in relation to the legislation of the different states. Perhaps the most extreme contrasts are provided by Beaver Run Schools and Kimberton Hills Village, both in Pennsylvania.

Beaver Run is an approved school, meeting standards of the state of Pennsylvania. It is licensed by the Department of Education's division of non-public schools, and each child from Pennsylvania is funded by the state. There must be a state-certified teacher in each classroom with a university degree in special education. A certain tension has developed between the philosophy of Camphill and that underlying the state regulations. The training course in curative education, offered by Camphill, is not acceptable to the state, and the college degrees of the teachers do not answer the needs of Camphill. However it is still possible to bridge the gap between the two through the work.

Kimberton Hills, as an agricultural community, does not fit into the Pennsylvania's existing legislation and has been allowed to exist on its own terms since 1972. It does not get financial aid from the state, but has received a grant from it to help formulate safeguards against the abuse, neglect and exploitation of people living in "life-sharing" situations not regulated by the state. Not having a licence has necessitated a continuous dialogue with those responsible for the administration of social services. Legislation may impose inertia as well as compliance, and Kimberton Hills feels that it is helping to foster new attitudes.

Opposite: Kimberton Hills, Pennsylvania. Bottom: Cheese-making, Kimberton Hills, Pennsylvania.

Maypole Dance and carnival at Beaver Run children's village, Pennsylvania (above). Camphill Village Ontario, Canada (below).

In New York State **Copake**, a Camphill village founded in 1961, has a population of over two hundred, about half of whom could be called retarded. The value of Camphill's work has been recognized by the Office of Mental Retardation and Developmental Disabilities, and new guidelines for the work have been formed in consultations between that Office and Camphill. The nearby "community of help" at **Triform** does not meet those guidelines and does not receive state help.

Camphill Village **Minnesota**, established in 1980, has been compelled to work within existing legislation and receives state help. The legislation makes it difficult to expand beyond the present population of thirty-six without new forms being found.

Camphill Village **Ontario**, fully established by 1987, works under Canadian law which is not as "advanced" as that in the United States.

The quality of the growth of the Camphill movement in North America is worthy of regard. It has involved a broad spectrum of society. Circles of human interest have formed around individuals in need of soul care, and around each centre. These circles include professionals, lawyers, and lay people, and have participated not only in the growth, but also in the decision-making, of each centre. They have attempted to grasp the essentials of Camphill, and this has allowed them to confirm their own experiences. It is this attempt that constitutes true growth, for it is based on an individual inner experience. It is this circle that is moving us towards forming an international or cosmopolitan legal body for the Camphill communities.

The social environment in which the Camphill villages grew has changed considerably since the 1960s when abuse of individual rights was widespread. The work with "retarded" people

lay at the centre of neglect, and, along with the Civil Rights Movement, was at the forefront of those groups pushing for change. At present, the most serious social challenge is substance abuse, and, through this, a lowering of social values. We will not be able to separate ourselves from these conditions and will have to discover how to bring healing to this social malaise.

Village choir in Fountain Hall, Copake, New York (completed in 1968).

The African region

South Africa

Julian Sleigh

What makes it relevant for Camphill to go to a country and set up communities? The ideas of Camphill attempt to uphold the dignity of man, and so one could say perhaps that wherever man is, Camphill is relevant. However, there is more to be considered. There must be the wish, indeed the will, of a group of people in the country to have Camphill take on a task within it. This is necessary, and indeed Camphill has never established a centre without first being asked. The entry of Camphill into any country calls for a finely-tuned dynamic process.

Camphill entered South Africa in 1957, following a call from a mother seven years earlier. Dr König had suggested that this parent, together with others similarly placed, should strive to found a centre for children in need of special care. During those seven years, this group developed a home just outside the small coastal town of **Hermanus** in the Cape Province, in an idyllic valley called Hemel-en-Aarde. In 1957 Dr König visited South Africa, lecturing and

Rankoromane School, Botswana.

meeting children, and acknowledged this centre as a Camphill place. Since then the work of Camphill has spread, through the support of more and more parents and the authorities. There are now three villages, a school and one small centre for individual care. These are the Camphill Village Alpha, fifty kilometres north of Cape Town; the school and farm community at Hermanus, 120 kilometres along the coast east of Cape Town; and the Cresset Camphill Community and the Novalis centre, halfway between Johannesburg and Pretoria.

Entering into South African society proved to be an entry into the white section of the population: but it was this group who had invited Camphill to come. Ever since establishing our centres, the question has lived among the co-workers: What can be done for the coloured and black people of this country? It was essential to wait for an invitation, for to be missionaries would have been unacceptable and, historically, unpardonable. Without an invitation nothing could be done. Yet we could not remain confined within our privileged population group.

A first step was to get to know the coloured and black culture, and to meet people at all levels belonging to these communities. We helped to form organizations that linked all the centres in the Western Cape and in the Johannesburg area working in the field of mental handicap. These organizations provided a forum that brought together people of all racial groups in training courses, special study groups and in working with parents. At a memorable gathering of parents at the City Hall in Cape Town in the early 1970s, a call came from prominent members of the coloured community to recognize the needs of that community. Straightaway a task force was formed for this purpose, and efforts were made to establish day-training centres in the various neighbourhoods of the coloured community. Camphill was not directly involved, but as convener of the task force I tried to ensure that a programme was

Camphill Village Alpha, South Africa (top left). Compare the soil now to the sandy soil when the village started in 1964 (right). Hermanus, Cape Province, South Africa (top right).

embarked upon that would bring about adequate services. The ideals that we uphold were fully accepted, so it was possible for these ideals to provide the basis for the whole programme.

Then, close to the Camphill village Alpha, north of Cape Town, a large area was designated to become a new town called Atlantis, for coloured people. Through our contact an action committee was formed in Atlantis, and the leaders of the group said at one meeting: "We want the Camphill model." Here was the invitation. We could not provide the workers ourselves, but we could work supportively and in a brotherly way with those who came from the people of Atlantis. These efforts resulted in the organization called **Orion**, which runs a large protected workshop, a training centre for school age children, and a special care centre. The local community and the authorities support this venture. It is not part of Camphill, but the director has been a Camphill co-worker for many years at Hemel-en-Aarde, Alpha and Cresset.

So far no similar development has taken place in the black communities, but the outreach has continued working actively with the national organization for the handicapped in South Africa. In regard to integration, we are severely hampered by our inability to speak the relevant African languages, and we have to bear in mind that for many black people, a European

lifestyle is strange and uncomfortable, especially if it has to be with white people. The social situation is highly complex. Cultural differences run deep, and we are still learning how deep they are. This makes for a rich diversity which begins to coalesce gradually as each group becomes more able to express itself on the national scene, but it will take a generation or more to lower the barriers. For us, the work in our own centres has been all-consuming, but we hope future efforts of Camphill will surmount these differences of culture and language. It is a long, hard road for all concerned.

The chapel (top) and dairy (above) at Camphill Village Alpha.

Camphill in South Africa endeavours to provide places where new methods of agriculture can be practised and demonstrated. The two villages in the Cape have poor sandy soil, and yet thriving farms have been established on both using bio-dynamic methods. Research projects have been initiated on crops that can withstand drought conditions in an area where rainfall is inadequate even in the rainy season. These crops provide feed for cattle and sheep, as well as oil for therapeutic and industrial use. Alongside these endeavours have been experiments in appropriate technology; trying to make use of natural resources to provide energy in order to save the expense of electricity and petrol.

Our centres have also become places where religion can be practised, and services and festivals celebrated in new forms that enhance community building and the growth of the individual. In this we work closely with The Christian Community.

We have tried to let the fruits of Anthroposophy provide seeds that could be planted in our centres. These seed-impulses need careful nurturing and growth to enable them to mature in the South African soil, but we believe that they are destined to serve the future of this country and contribute towards making it a more peaceful land.

Camphill in Botswana

Werner Groth

Botswana is a country full of contradictions. Independent since 1966, it is said to be the only functioning democracy in Africa. Half the country is covered by the arid Kalahari Desert, and yet in the north there is the huge Okavango Delta which swells and fills every year with the seasonal rains in Angola.

The same contrasts hold true for the people of Botswana. The majority live in rural areas in simple houses, often mud huts, stamping sorghum in wooden bowls and cooking porridge in a three-legged pot over an open fire.

Doctors practising traditional medicine try to help the people solve their problems in their own way, though there are many health posts built by the government. Then there is the town population with trained, sophisticated people who run an efficient if bureaucratic administration with computers, fax machines and the protocol of diplomatic services.

156

Camphill started its school, **Rankoromane**, in 1974 and it has grown to house forty-five physically, mentally or multiple handicapped children. Their families are often quite sympathetic to their problems, but usually quite unable to help. The children are receptive in quite a unique way, especially to the substance of the Waldorf curriculum, although it has had to be adapted to the culture of the people.

There have been twelve Botswana women working for many years with the children in the Camphill Community who identify with Camphill and its attitude towards the handicapped child.

Helping hands in classroom work. Throughout Camphill schools children are taught on the basis of the Waldorf School curriculum (for normal children). In Camphill the curriculum for all twelve classes from primary through to secondary schooling is adapted to the special needs of children with developmental disabilities.

Several day schools have been started in villages in other parts of the country. These were then taken over by the district administrations. The government will only support a school for six years, so it was decided to develop workshops to support as much of the running costs of the school as possible. This was not only quite successful financially, but also created a very strong public awareness of Camphill and its aims, especially since a large shop was opened in the capital.

There are now plans for a Camphill village in Botswana as some of our ex-pupils find it impossible to find any meaningful work and a socially acceptable living space in the society.

Carnival celebration,
Angaia Camphill, Brazil.

South America: Camphill in Brazil

Nico Brodnitz

Brazil is a mystical country full of the forces of nature, surrounded by the elements of fire and water, it is known for its birds, butterflies, flowers, and big trees which have little roots. The splendour of nature and the joyful energy of the people are well represented in the Brazilian carnival. The Brazilian folk soul can, perhaps, be compared to the soul of a child. Populated by an amazingly diverse mixture of people from very different racial backgrounds there is altogether a completely different mentality from Central Europe. The people are ingenuous, but also cunning; warm-hearted, but superficial; quite disorganized, but marvellous at improvising.

Into this vibrant environment, Camphill Angaià was born in 1979 in Campos do Jordao (commonly known as the Brazilian Switzerland). Gunda Müller-Bay began the work, and Angaià started when several young Brazilians joined her after finishing their curative education training in Europe.

It was felt that Angaià needed a more typically Brazilian surrounding and identity, and eventually the presence of a group of anthroposophical doctors and the offer of land by the

159

Angaià, about 160 km (100 miles) north of Rio de Janiero, is the only Camphill community at this time in South America. This isolation presents a challenge in creating living and active links to other Camphill regions.

mayor of Juiz de Fora, a city three hours north of Rio de Janiero, led to Angaià's move there in 1981.

The new life came as a shock to everyone. Co-workers and volunteers, used to modern luxuries, were confronted with the day to day reality of no electricity, running water, post or telephone. The same Mother Nature who provided trees weighed down with banana, avocado or mango, could also decide to make the only public road so muddy as to be impassable after a week of incessant rain. There were frequently days when there was not much food on the table. The site had one house and several shacks, yet in the middle of all this was a swimming pool, typifying the paradoxical extremes of the country.

Among all the polarities is the reversal of the seasons. With festivals such as Christmas celebrated in the heat of summer, new forms must be found for their celebration. The greatest spiritual support for Angaià came from the regular Sunday service, and in many a difficult situation this is what carried the co-workers through, giving renewed strength and perseverance for the work. Angaià, meaning "healthy soul" in a Brazilian Indian language, began to bring healing to the land and the spiritual environment as well as to those placed in its care.

Another challenging aspect is money. To deal with finances in a country that has at times inflation running at twenty per cent a month, without help from the government, is a full-time job in itself.

In 1984 with the help of many friends, another nineteen-hectare site was purchased and developed. This gave the basis for farm work and was a great step towards self-sufficiency. Yet it is a long way before Angaià is able to stand on its own two feet.

Angaià today is like a child looking forward to its first day at school; full of anticipation for the future. Its development, because of the difficulties of moving and adapting, has taken time. But, like a child, it is keen to learn and has much to look forward to. Angaià looks forward to a future full of promise and hope in which the South American continent may provide a home for many new initiatives.

Chapter 6

Community building towards the future

Leonardo Fulgosi

One of the most difficult things to understand about the Camphill movement is how it can be co-ordinated without a central administrative council. It is also one of its most modern characteristics. The development of Camphill has not been directed by laws, charters and regulations dictated from a central institution. Every school or village community within the Camphill movement has adapted itself to the characteristics, requirements and organizations of the country in which it exists. Each place appears to be entirely autonomous. Even in the same country individual structures and forms have evolved which are capable of operating independently. The problems of internal organization, of recruiting co-workers or staff, of admitting children, adolescents and adults, and the solution of financial problems, as well as the various aspects of social life within the community, are solved by each school or village community in its own way.

The Camphill movement concentrates on the principles of social organization which permit each one of its participants to be integrated fully into social life. Consideration of the social or human, economic and cultural dimensions in the "body social", as separate but inextricably related components, provides the ground on which the building of our communities takes place. This aspect (referred to in Chapter 3) constitutes a major part of Camphill. It leads to the integration of each personality as an equal among equals, irrespective of illness, race or other differences. These two factors — the threefold structuring of social life and the recognition of each person as an equal — are mutually supportive and play a vital role in the social life of Camphill.

The Camphill movement has gone beyond building schools and villages in which children and adults can find a way to social integration. It has begun to create social structures which foster a harmonization of different and differing personalities within the changing stream of time.

The effort to integrate diverse personalities, some with handicapping conditions, as equals among equals, is *not* dependent on physical environment. An urban, suburban or rural environment is equally suitable to this kind of relationship. Social achievements, no matter how small, create the territory for the building of community life. The fundamental principles which regulate the forms of social life and relationships are based on a recognition of the natural threefold organization of social life into the human concerns (legal and rights) sphere, the economic realm, and the whole area of cultural, educational and spiritual activity. Thus, it is the effort to establish relationships of equality in the *regulation* of work, of developing fraternity and co-operation in the exploration and activity of economic life, and maintaining complete freedom and independence in the cultural, educational and spiritual endeavours which contribute to a more precise understanding of social life.

This idea of community life has developed tremendously since the early days of Camphill. Numerous schools and villages have been created, and the contribution to the continuing search for viable answers to the social question has been not only accepted but also taken up with gratitude in many parts of the world.

Other ways have been found to bring the ideas of community life into existence. The concept of village life and community building has been reinforced to resolve questions of integration and human dignity regarding the individual with handicaps. The person who presents physical or psychological impediments or who has suffered disturbances in childhood has been recognized as a full person equal to others; a brother or sister to each human being. It is essential that the individuality develop freely and to the fullest possible extent, so that the true being of that person may manifest. The principle of human integrity — or manifestation of individual being — belongs to the great ideal of humanity.

This principle is at the same time a call to our humanity by those born with a destiny which makes them dependent on other people. The eternal image of the child has been central to the development and expansion of the Camphill movement. It is also an image which could guide us towards an understanding that every human being is in the process of becoming. This path of development, of becoming, this evolution of mankind, can perhaps be understood through research on questions of human destiny (particularly such as are revealed through people with handicaps). This can be seen in the larger and greater view of human existence which goes beyond birth and death, and reaches into the realm of reincarnation.

With such questions one is brought to the impulse of healing. Seen in its larger context, healing relates directly to social life. For true healing to occur a real interest in the other person must exist; an interest that can be likened to the attempt to recognize one another as equals among equals in social life. This human interest is of the same kind, whether as a basis for healing or for the establishment of a social organism. Indeed, there are many similarities between the healing impulse and a healthy social life! It is these similarities that have been of particular interest to Camphill.

Mutual care in the realm of physical existence and the care which goes from soul to soul will create new connections between people through which the old bonds produced by blood ties or the politics of nations will be transcended. Our real "home" is increasingly seen to be the world, our earth. This awareness has partially contributed to the growing consciousness of being a world-wide movement. The forces of cohesion in Camphill are not physical, outer arrangements, but are related to the spiritual striving for an ideal. The human being can learn ever more about the spirit in the discovery of the physical world. We can recognize ourselves as individuals, but also as related to and dependent on other human beings.

Throughout Camphill's development research in spiritual science, particularly related to community building and social life, has been of paramount importance (see Chapter 3, Camphill and Anthroposophy). Camphill's has not been a random development or mere conglomeration of activities.

This book presents some of the elements which have contributed to the growth of the community building efforts of Dr Karl König. One could not just offer a glorious or self-serving picture of Camphill. Indeed, our failures and weaknesses can be experienced equally. They are evident in much of what we do. Nevertheless, the process of becoming, of striving and growing, contains the risk of error and failure. However, these are also the stimuli to reach with renewed force and enthusiasm toward the aims and ideals.

The ideal community of the future will ground itself on the objective force of love which is the light of Christ, the healer of the world. The force of cohesion for the building of community life in the effort to heal the earth and the social organism is, and will be more so in the future, love — without discrimination, without reservation. Only with the warmth of love can humankind accomplish its mission; find the light which will bring healing to its full realization. Man can begin to find the way to this light. Mankind has already perceived the tender light which will burn in hearts everywhere in the future. Today, Camphill offers its contribution in the image of a candle which has begun to burn in the work, life and the growth of many, many, children, adolescents and adults.

Notes on contributors

Cornelius Pietzner, born in Camphill Northern Ireland, was raised in Camphill in the United States, where he has varied responsibilities. He edited *Village Life*, a photographic documentary of Camphill in America, published in 1986.

Christof-Andreas Lindenberg, Beaver Run, United States, has been involved with Camphill for over forty years in both schools and villages.

Friedwart Bock is a principal of the Camphill Schools, Aberdeen, and is responsible for the development of Camphill in Great Britain.

Henning Hansmann has been active in the development of Camphill for several decades. Until recently he was principal of the Camphill Schools, Aberdeen, Scotland, where he still resides.

Barbara Lipsker, Northern Ireland, is one of the pioneers of the Camphill Movement, and now lives at Glencraig Camphill Community.

Penelope Roberts, New York, came to Camphill as a young adult and has lived and worked in Copake Village for nearly twenty years.

Peter Roth, a founder member of Camphill, is a priest of The Christian Community. He has been active in the "village work" and has made his home in Botton Village, England, since its inception in the mid-1950s.

Deborah Hudson is involved in the work of the youth groups, and is editor of *Camphill Correspondence*. She lives in Middlesbrough, England.

Karen von Schilling is a pioneer of the work in South Africa where she has lived for many years. Her general anthroposophical work has taken her to many other parts of Africa.

Christoph Jensen is a farmer living in Alpha, South Africa.

Leonardo Fulgosi has worked in Camphill as a physician and is responsible for many aspects of the movement's development, particularly in Central Europe.

Map
of Camphill
centres

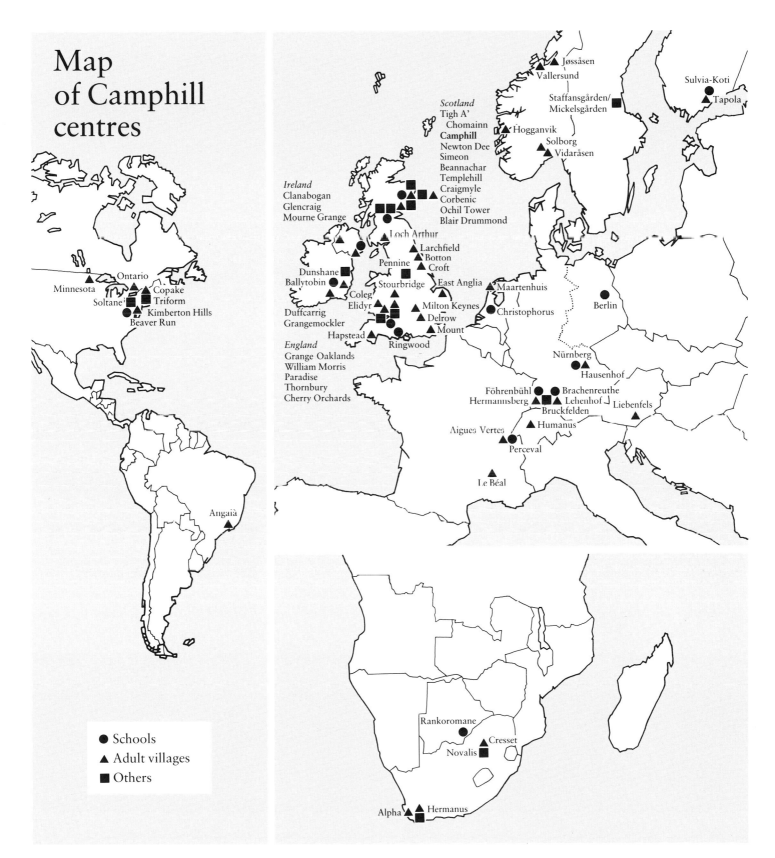

Minnesota
Ontario
Soltane
Copake
Triform
Kimberton Hills
Beaver Run

Angaià

Ireland
Clanabogan
Glencraig
Mourne Grange

Dunshane
Ballytobin

Duffcarrig
Grangemockler

England
Grange Oaklands
William Morris
Paradise
Thornbury
Cherry Orchards

Scotland
Tigh A'
Chomainn
Camphill
Newton Dee
Simeon
Beannachar
Templehill
Craigmyle
Corbenic
Ochil Tower
Blair Drummond

Loch Arthur
Larchfield
Botton
Croft
Pennine
Stourbridge
East Anglia
Coleg
Elidyr
Milton Keynes
Delrow
Hapstead
Mount
Ringwood

Jøssåsen
Vallersund
Staffansgården/
Mickelsgården
Hogganvik
Solborg
Vidaråsen
Sulvia-Koti
Tapola

Maartenhuis
Christophorus
Berlin
Nürnberg
Hausenhof
Föhrenbühl
Brachenreuthe
Hermannsberg
Lehenhof
Bruckfelden
Liebenfels
Humanus
Aigues Vertes
Perceval
Le Béal

Rankoromane
Cresset
Novalis
Alpha
Hermanus

● Schools
▲ Adult villages
■ Others

Contact addresses

The following is a condensed list of Camphill centres. For more information about the Camphill communities in each country, contact the centres listed below:

Austria: Camphill Liebenfels, 9556 Liebenfels
Botswana: Camphill Community Rankoromane, PO Box 34, Otse
Brazil: Angaià Camphill do Brasil, CP 1122, 36100 Juiz de Fora, MG
Canada: Camphill Village Ontario, RR1, Angus, Ont. L0M 1B0
England: Botton Village, Danby, Whitby, North Yorkshire YO21 2NJ
      Sheiling Schools, Thornbury Park, Thornbury, Bristol BS12 1HP
Finland: Sylvia-Koti, 16999 Lahti
France: Foyer de Vie, Le Béal, 26770 Taulignan
Germany: Heimsonderschule Föhrenbühl, 7799 Heiligenberg
Ireland: Camphill Village Community Duffcarrig, Gorey, Co. Wexford
Northern Ireland: Glencraig Camphill Community, Craigavad, Holywood, Co. Down BT18
      0DB
Netherlands: Stichting Christophorus, Duinweg 35, 3735 LC Bosch en Duin
Norway: Vidaråsen Landsby, 3240 Andebu
Scotland: Camphill Rudolf Steiner Schools, Murtle, Bieldside, Aberdeen AB1 9EP
      Newton Dee Village Community, Bieldside, Aberdeen AB1 9DX
South Africa: Camphill Village Alpha, 7302 Kalbaskraal, Western Cape
Sweden: Staffansgården, Furugatan 1, 820 60 Delsbo
Switzerland: Perceval, Route de Lussy, 1162 St Prex
U S A: Camphill Soltane, Box 300A, RD1, Glenmoore, PA 19343
      Camphill Village, Copake, NY 12516
Wales: Coleg Elidyr, Rhandirmwyn, Llandovery, Dyfed, SA20 0NL

Photographic Acknowledgements

Jeff Balls 157 top left
Ernst-Dieter Berthold 134 (all)
Roland Bienoth 81 top, centre
Paul Bock 72, 81 bottom, 86 right, 90 (all)
Eva Dilg 135 (both), 136 top right & bottom
Georg Domeier 83 left, 129, 131, 136 top left, 138, 139 (all), 140 bottom
J. Greene 152 top right
Terje Halvorsen 145 bottom right
J. Holbeck 99, 100 left, 103 left, 105
Thomas Horan 122, 126 top & bottom right, 128 top
Humanus Haus 74 top left
Jerry Irwin 150 top, 151 (both), 152 top left
David Joiner 145 top
Nils Langeland 141, 142, 143 top left & bottom
J. Lappalainer 147 top
Leslie Lawson 153 bottom, 156 (all), 157 top right & bottom, 158 (both)
Andrew Layfield 145 top & bottom left
Günther Lehr 46 top
Boris Moscoff 80, 83 right, 84, 92 bottom
Regina McCarthy 123, 124 left, 126 bottom left
T. McNally 155 top
Manfred Maier 153 top right
Ursel Pietzner 49 bottom
Nick Poole 73, 74 top right & bottom, 76, 77, 78, 79, 82 (both), 89 (both), 92 top, 100 right, 108, 110
     (all), 111, 112, 113, 114, 116 (both), 117 top, 119, 121 (both), 125, 137, 147 bottom, 148 (both)
Stephan Rash 149, 152 bottom
Sy Rudges 153 top left
Julian Sleigh 154 top left, left margin & bottom, 155 centre
Bruno Wegmuller 86 left, 130, 132 (both)

Index

(*Italics* refer to photographs, **bold** figures refer to authors)